Fearless

FINDING COURAGE IN THE CHARACTER OF GOD

GRANT GRAVES

ISBN: 978-1-7356683-0-7 (Paperback)

Cover Design by 100Covers.com
Interior Design by FormattedBooks.com

DEDICATION

This book is dedicated to Dr. Jan Haluska.

You taught me how to write, how to teach,
and how to never give up.

This book is for you, Dr. Haluska.

May we all have clean desks and pure hearts.

CONTENTS

*The path to learning wanders
through a good story.*
—Grant Graves

PREFACE

Do you have a dream? Do you have an image of who you would be if you could be anyone? Do you believe that you were made to do something special?

I believe that God plants dreams in our hearts like a farmer plants seeds. Then He waters our dreams with encouragement and shines down on us with love. I believe that one of His greatest joys is to see the dreams of His children come true.

For as long as I can remember it has been my dream to write a book. It took years to find a topic that felt worthy of the time it would take for me to write a book and for people to read it.

My spiritual journey has taken many twists and turns, but over the last decade, God has gently taught me many things. I used to love God but was still afraid of Him. I tried so hard to be good enough, and I kept failing. Now I understand that

God is good enough, so I don't have to be. I just need to trust Him.

While many Christians say they trust in God, most of us have a hard time putting into practice the things we hear in church. What I have discovered is that there are certain deep rooted beliefs in Christianity that instill a quiet fear of God. When these beliefs are pulled up and laid out in the sunshine, they seem so ugly that we wonder how we ever could have believed them.

This book is my attempt to pull up some weeds and plant some seeds. Jesus loved to tell stories, and I followed His example. In sharing familiar tales, I have done my best to remain faithful to biblical facts and the spirit of the stories. While striving to maintain accuracy, I added some details to move the story along, filled in descriptions where the Bible was silent, and attempted to portray the heroes of the Bible in a way that made them seem very much like you and me. Each story has a footnote, so you can go straight to the source. I have also quoted many Scripture verses by combining several translations. My goal was to capture the essence of the verse and touch the heart of the reader. For each Bible text footnote, I included the Bible translation or if I based the verse on multiple translations.

The goal of this book is simple. I want you to see Jesus. I want your fears to melt away and reveal the heart of courage that Jesus has seen all along. I am here to point up and say, "Look! The Lamb of God is here to heal your hearts!"

If you see God in a way that awakens a love for Him, if you decide to trust Jesus with your heart, or if you take one step closer to believing that God is truly good, then my dream will have come true.

May God bless you as you read this book. May He guide you into truth and shine His warm light into the dark corners of your soul. May God's love transform you into someone who is loving, someone who is kind, and someone who is fearless.

Chapter 1

THE TRANSFORMATION

"God sent His Son into the world
not to judge it, but to save it."[1]
—Jesus

"Anyone who belongs to Christ has
become a new person. The old life
is gone; a new life has begun!"[2]
— Paul

The Trap

She was sound asleep when the door crashed open.
Two burly men rushed inside yelling. They tore the
sheets from the bed and grabbed her. She screamed
in terror and kicked at her assailants. She reached

---

1   John 3:17 NLT
2   2 Corinthians 5:17

for the man who had been asleep next to her, but he had rolled away. She clawed at a sheet and tried to cover her naked body as they dragged her across the bed.

"You whore!" the men hissed. "You'll pay for this!" Then they threw her to the floor. She landed hard and cried out in pain. Then she frantically grabbed the crumpled sheets and pulled them quickly around her bare skin. *This can't be happening!* she thought, too terrified to make a sound as tears streamed down her face.

Then the priest entered the room, and the chaos calmed. The men who had been trashing the room froze; their harsh voices dropped to a whisper. The priest's smug eyes took in the room and knew what had happened.

The small table still had a few leftovers from dinner the night before. A spent candle stood next to a bouquet of wildflowers. A trail of clothes led from the table across a colorful mat and ended next to the bed. The priest's eyes narrowed as he glared at a young man who had jumped out of the bed and was fumbling with a tunic. Shame colored the man's cheeks, and his downcast eyes betrayed his guilt. The priest's hard face broke into an evil smile. The plan was working perfectly. The priest's lips curled in disdain as he reached into his robe and pulled out a small pouch of money.

"For your services," the holy man snarled and tossed the pouch across the room to the red faced man. He caught it, and everyone heard the clink of coins.

Then the priest slid his attention to the young woman huddled on the floor at his feet. His heart lurched, and the priest's jaw dropped. The rumors about her beauty had failed to prepare him for the sight of her now. She was absolutely gorgeous. He forced himself to regain his composure, but he could not tear his eyes away from her beauty.

Her thick, brown hair fell across her face while the smooth curves of her body barely hid beneath the thin sheet. A delicate hand slid a lock of hair behind her ear, and the priest's wanton stare caught a glimpse of forbidden flesh. The woman's moist, round lips quivered, and her dark eyes flashed as she looked past the priest to the man counting his coins. Sharp shivers of desire ran through the holy man's body.

But the stunning woman failed to notice the priest's deep interest in her appearance. She saw only one man, her lover who had become her betrayer. As he dropped the coins one by one into the pouch, she noticed the wildflowers on the table and choked back her tears. *Why?* she kept asking herself.

The woman closed her eyes, remembering the last few days. She shook her head and sighed. He had been charming, attentive, and romantic, and she foolishly let herself be swept away with his tender touches and loving whispers. As his lips brushed hers, he promised to take her away and make her his wife. When his kisses grew passionate, she had let him lead her to the bed. She raised her head and watched the hands that had warmly caressed her the night before, now cooly count coins.

How stupid I am! She bowed her head in shame as the haunting voices came flooding back. Her mother's disappointed voice echoed from the past, "Mary! Why can't you be more like your sister?" Then she heard her sister's sharp tongue, "No man will ever love you now. Not after what you've done." But the last accusation cut the deepest. The disgusted voice of her father thundered in her head. "I can't believe my daughter turned out to be like you."

Mary winced as the words sliced fresh wounds. Her stomach twisted in pain, and she clenched her fists. *They were right!* Mary agonized. *I'll never be good enough! No matter how hard I try, all I end up doing is making it worse. I am so stupid and worthless.*

"You may leave now," the priest's harsh voice ripped through Mary's thoughts. She glanced up, hoping he was talking to her, but he wasn't. The priest faced the man Mary thought loved her, pointed to the open door, and then lowered his voice, "But remember, not a word, or you'll end up where we found you."

Mary watched the young man cross the room toward the open door. He stepped over the clothes he had so gently slid off her shoulders the night before and stopped in front of Mary. For a long moment he stared at the table where the wildflowers lay.

Mary's heart skipped a beat. Would he help her now? He could still rescue her. All he had to do was say, "Let her go!" or even grab her hand, and they could run away together.

He took a deep breath and finally looked down at Mary. Their eyes met, and she silently pleaded for help. His jaw twitched, and his lips quivered. But then he blinked and looked away. He said nothing as he stepped over her and disappeared out the door.

Mary's heart shattered. The footsteps of her last hope faded, and Mary's blood turned cold as she realized how completely alone she was. There was no one who would speak up for her, defend her, or save her. She was abandoned, betrayed, and doomed to die for her sins.

"My dear, do you know the penalty for adultery?" the priest asked as he squatted down and peered into Mary's face. He refocused all his lust and desire for her into bitter disdain. "You are a sinner, an utter disgrace to your family, your community, and to our holy nation. God commands that you be judged and stoned to death."

Mary stared at the floor and tried to breathe. She felt a dark weight pressing down on her. Blood pounded in her forehead, and her vision blurred. Nausea churned in her stomach, and Mary thought she was going to throw up. She saw her many sins and knew the consequences for breaking God's law. *He's right*, she thought. *I deserve death.*

"Get up, you wretch," the priest's voice dripped with venom. Then he snickered, "Take her to the Teacher."

The men who had thrown her to the floor now seized her roughly and lifted Mary to her feet. She clutched the flimsy sheet to her chest and tried desperately to wrap it around her naked body as the men dragged her out of the house and into the bright sunlight. This was her judgment day.

The Teacher

The crisp morning air nipped at Mary's bare skin, but it was the shame that sent chills down her back. Sharp rocks cut her feet as she stumbled and tried not to fall. Everything was a blur. The thin sheet kept slipping down, exposing Mary's body for all to see. Priests and Pharisees mysteriously emerged from dark doorways and narrow alleys. She noticed more people joining the procession, eager to watch the spectacle. Mary didn't discern their smug looks and secretive nods. Soon, twenty or so men marched alongside her. They glared at Mary, and she winced as another rock cut into her heel. Mary cried out in pain, but could not slow her pace.

Then Mary heard the voices. Someone called her name, and she quickly turned away from the familiar faces. Mary's cheeks burned with shame, and she pulled the fabric tighter around her shoulders, trying to shield herself from the painful words.

"Is that Deborah's girl?"

"I knew she would end up like this."

"Such a disappointment."

"Thank God her parents are dead."

Mary tried to shut out the words, the guilt, the shame, but they washed over her. She could barely breathe, and her vision turned blurry and dark. She was about to lose consciousness, when suddenly they stopped.

"Get out of our way!" the angry priest shouted. "We are on God's business!" He elbowed his way through a large crowd of people gathered in front of a smiling Teacher. The Man was sitting on the back of a cart, and several children played at His feet and sat on His lap. The priests halted in front of the Teacher. The smile and the children disappeared.

"Bring out the adulterous woman!" the priest ordered.

The crowd parted back in horror as if Mary was a leper, and rough hands threw her forward and shoved her to the ground in front of the cart. Pain seared through her body as the ground tore at her knees and shoulder. The sheet slipped off, and Mary heard whistles and gasps of disgust. She frantically pulled it back over her bare skin. Disgraced and ashamed, Mary curled into a tight ball and welcomed death.

"Well, Jesus," the priest called out loudly. "I hate to interrupt your fascinating story, but my fellow priests and I need your help." The group of leaders and teachers of the law pushed their way forward and exchanged knowing glances.

The priest pointed his finger directly at Mary's cowering form. "This woman, this worm was caught in the very act of adultery." He paused smugly as the crowd murmured their disapproval. "We all know the importance of God's holy commandments. We also know of God's righteous wrath for the sinners who dare to disobey. Today we must honor our holy God with true justice."

The priest's shrill voice rose over the noise of the marketplace, and soon the entire square fell silent. The priest walked in slow circles around Mary, like a lion yearning to pounce. Then he smiled slightly, motioning toward Jesus.

"We are so blessed to have this honorable and wise rabbi from Nazareth among us." The priest stopped his pacing, stood directly in front of Jesus, and then folded his arms.

"Now although you never went to the synagogue schools, surely you are familiar with the seventh commandment: Thou shalt not commit adultery." The priest sneered and then bent down to pick up a large rock.

The priest cleared his throat and spoke louder, "The law of Moses is quite clear. Justice demands that we stone this adulterer to death and cleanse this sin from our community. But the Romans don't quite see it that way and refuse to let us obey our own laws." He glanced at Mary. Hatred turned his eyes smoky black. Then the priest gave Jesus a mock bow. He rose, tossed the rock up into the air, and caught it.

"What do you say, Jesus?" The priest leaned forward. "Should we obey God or the Romans?"

Captivated, the crowd stared at Jesus. He sat on the cart wearing the simple clothes of a peasant, yet His nobility gave Him the look of a king. Jesus closed His eyes, bowed His head, and was silent. Taking His calm silence as permission, the priests and Pharisees picked up large rocks. Others quickly followed, and the mood of the crowd turned sinister.

Mary sensed her death was near and shuddered. She hugged her arms and curled even tighter, bracing herself for the first impact. Mary could almost hear the stones whistling through the air. She thought about praying but quickly rejected that idea. God would not help her. She had knowingly and deliberately broken God's holy commandment, so now she must accept His justice. God was disgusted with her and would never answer her plea for mercy. She was alone, afraid, and hopeless. Mary caught her breath and tried to stop crying.

"Rabbi," the priest taunted. "We are all waiting for your judgment?" He huffed impatiently and started to speak, but Jesus pushed Himself up off the cart. His feet landed firmly on the ground, scattering a few stones. Jesus moved and stood directly between Mary and the crowd. His penetrating eyes flashed with power. The priest took a step back, and arms poised to throw stones dropped to their sides.

Mary heard the thud of Jesus' feet as they landed on the ground and came closer to where she huddled. Her judge had not yet spoken a single word, but when Mary heard Jesus bending over, she knew He was picking up a stone. Mary held her breath, waiting for His just condemnation, waiting for Him to throw the first rock.

But no harsh sentence thunderd above her, instead Mary heard a strange scraping sound. Bewildered, she opened one eye. Jesus was holding a stick and scribbling in the sand near her feet.

"Well?" the priest folded his hands. "It seems as if Jesus is speechless. He would rather play in the dirt than make important decisions. What kind of a judge would—"

"Look!" someone interrupted. "He's writing something." The crowd edged closer.

Jesus paused and then stood. His voice, clear and strong, echoed over the curious crowd.

"All right," Jesus said. "Let the one who has never sinned throw the first stone." Then He leaned over and continued to write.

Mary clenched her eyes shut and gritted her teeth. She was going to die. The Teacher's death sentence hung over her, and every muscle tensed as she waited for the first stone to slam into her body.

But nothing happened.

Moments passed. Mary started to breath again. She heard a soft thump. Slowly she opened her eyes and saw fists clutching stones all around her. She watched as someone unclenched his hand and dropped his stone. The rock hit the ground and rolled toward her as the man disappeared. More stones hit the ground. More people slunk away.

"What kind of trickery is this?" the priest demanded. He stomped over to where Jesus was writing and looked down. The priest read the words scribbled in the sand. A sharp gasp of air escaped his lips, and Mary heard him whisper, "How could you know?"

The priest stepped back in disbelief and looked at Jesus with horror. The priest's face blanched, and he unexpectedly dropped his rock and fled.

Others pushed forward to read the words scrawled near Mary's feet, and each left in quiet shame. Soon Mary couldn't see anyone standing in front of her.

Jesus never stopped writing until all the rocks had fallen and most of the crowd had retreated. He deeply sighed and looked at the stick in His hand. He tossed it away and then placed His hands in the dirt. With broad, strong strokes, Jesus' hand smoothed the sand, erasing each word. He brushed His dusty hands together and turned to Mary.

She was sitting now, still shaking under her frail sheet, but her quick eyes followed His every move. Mary sensed Jesus' gentle nobility and quiet strength.

The purity of His presence made her keenly aware of her sins, but at the same time she felt drawn to its warmth. Somehow Mary knew Jesus wasn't going to pick up a stone. She looked into His compassionate eyes, and in that brief moment, Jesus read her soul. Every secret, every shame rose to the surface of her heart, and the darkness of her sins threatened to overwhelm her. Mary blinked back hot tears of remorse, but she held Jesus' gaze. Instead of disgust, His face showed genuine, profound love, the kind of love that Mary had always yearned for but never experienced.

Jesus shifted His weight and took off His outer cloak. He held it out toward her.

"Here," Jesus said gently. "Take my robe and put it on."

Mary held the sheet to herself with one hand and with the other reached out and took the cloak. Jesus' eyes never wavered but stayed locked on hers.

Mary wrapped Jesus' cloak tightly around her thin shoulders. The heavy warmth of His robe felt safe. For the first time that morning, she was covered. Mary didn't understand such compassionate, gracious love.

Jesus sat down in the dirt and gestured to the now empty square. "Where is everyone?" He asked softly. "Where are your accusers?"

Mary wiped her nose and glanced around the marketplace. The priests and Pharisees, the men who had hauled her here, and the judgmental crowd had vanished. Relief flooded through her, and the tears came again.

"They are gone, my Lord," she whispered between sobs.

"Mary," Jesus said. She stopped and looked directly into Jesus's kind eyes. What she saw there astonished her. It was something she never saw in her father's eyes or heard in her mother's voice. She saw complete and utter acceptance.

Jesus held her gaze and spoke, "I am here to show you God's love, His forgiveness, and to remind you that you are His child."

Jesus paused and let His words sink into Mary's heart. "God will never betray or abandon you, Mary. He loves you too much." Her thirsty heart soaked up Jesus' words of hope.

"God has sent Me to heal you, to save you," Jesus said quietly. He stood up and held out His hand.

Mary took Jesus' hand and stood slowly to her feet. Jesus' words echoed into the dark places in her soul. Although her body ached and a sharp sting shot through her knees, her physical pain barely registered. The deep anguish in her soul was gone. Mary smiled and squeezed Jesus' hand. She looked without fear or shame directly into Jesus' kind eyes and whispered, "Thank you."

Jesus smiled, "Mary, I am not here to condemn you."

A New Beginning

As Mary limped out of the marketplace, she repeated Jesus's words over and over again, "I am not here to condemn you. I am not here to condemn you." *What kind of prophet was this? What kind of God was He talking about?*

Jesus could have condemned her, but instead He set her free. Jesus could have punished her, but instead He forgave her completely. *What kind of justice is this?* Mary wondered. She placed her hand over her heart and realized that all her cold fear and burning shame was gone. In its place, for the first time, Mary felt only a deep sense of warm peace.

Mary smiled and cinched Jesus' robe tighter around her waist as she strode past the street leading to her old apartment and her old life. Instead she chose a different path, another road leading to a fresh new life.

Soon Mary had walked out the city gates and into the green countryside. She took a deep breath of fresh air and felt clean. She was ready to face her past and her family. Mary turned down a sideroad and began to climb up a familiar hill. It had been a long time since she had run away from home. Back then, she had been a scared girl, full of anger, fear, and shame. But now she was different.

Jesus had healed Mary. Her heart was full of His peace, courage, and purity. She knew that no matter what happened, everything would be okay because of Jesus. Mary didn't know why she felt that way, but she knew in her heart that everything had changed. She could stop running from her past. She could stop searching for love in the arms of men. She could start to make things right. It was time to go home. It was time to begin a new life.[3]

Sticks and Stones

Do you ever feel like Mary? Afraid? Ashamed? Full of despair? Do the accusing voices whisper in your ear? *You'll never be good enough. You are a failure. God can't love you.*

The sharp voice of the priest echoes in our hearts as we look at our sins strewn across the floor and sink down into hopelessness. Our good deeds and well-meaning behavior feel like a thin sheet barely wrapped around our naked souls. We know we deserve the stones, and we wonder if God could ever love us, forgive us, or heal our brokenness. We hear the promise of Judgment Day and shrink away from the stern God of justice, who looms over us— austere, strict, and tough. In His holy shadow, we feel lost, alone, and afraid.

I have those dark days, those dark thoughts. I can preach and teach and look good on the outside, but many days, my cold fear claws just below the surface. I'm afraid of rejection and failure, so I try hard to be good enough. I jump through the hoops

---

3   John 8:1-11

and talk a good talk. But when I yell at my daughter or lose my temper, the doubts come rushing in and throw me to my knees. Like Mary, I wonder if I am good enough for God.

I grew up in the Bible Belt. I had a great home with supportive parents and a warm church family. I went to Christian schools and aced the Bible trivia games, but even though I knew the stories and the memory verses, there was always an underlying fear of a vengeful God. I was afraid of dying, of Judgment Day, of meeting God face to face. I knew I wasn't good enough, and I was afraid that God would judge me and send me to hell.

We are too familiar with our sins and faults. Church often makes us feel worse. We put on masks and fig leaves trying to pretend we are living victoriously when in reality we had a huge argument in the car on the way to church. We smile and nod and hide our depression or anxiety. We lift our hands in praise and hide addictions in our hearts. We go to church hoping to be refreshed with living water, but we leave parched, disappointed, and disillusioned with our inability to live up to our own standards. We feel burdened by the call to study our Bible better or witness to our neighbors or give more money to the church. The God preached from many pulpits seems more interested in perfect people and dusty rules than messy lives and turbulent hearts like mine.

The Familiar Sermon

The pastor was good. He knew how to grab his audience's attention. He started with a funny story and then hit the congregation with a zinger of truth.

Loud amens and murmurs of approval rolled over the pews. The pastor was getting warmed up. He blazed through a couple of familiar Bible verses and dove into another story. Then he surprised everyone with new insight. It was almost lunch time, but no one cared. He was that good.

Then the pastor described God. He painted a picture of a loving father, a devoted friend, and a merciful savior. He leaned over the pulpit and begged the believers to look at the cross. He pointed to the tall stained glass image of Jesus holding out His hands as if calling us to follow Him.

The pastor rose to a crescendo of passion, then he stopped. He slowly took out a handkerchief and dabbed his forehead. Everyone waited for his next words. The pastor had the congregation in the palm of his hand, and he knew it.

"Today is the day, my friends," he began. "Today is the day you can step into eternity. You can take the outstretched hands of Jesus and say 'yes' to your Savior."

He looked over his people and asked, "Do you want peace?"

"Yes!" they responded.

"Do you want to walk those streets of gold and sing with the angel choir?" his enthusiasm grew.

"Yes! Preach it!" someone called out.

"Then stand up and be counted, for the hour of judgment is near! My friends, we don't know how much time we have, and if we pass up on this opportunity, if we walk away from Jesus, then what will happen if we don't live to meet together next week?" The pastor continued with energy. "Remember that God is forgiving!"

"Amen!" they chanted.

"God is merciful!" he shouted.

"Hallelujah!" they cried.

"God is love!" He belted it out with a boom.

The people stood to their feet and clapped their hands. Amens and hallelujahs echoed from the rafters.

Then the pastor stepped out from behind his pulpit, and his voice got low. "God is all those things, my friends. But—"

Then he paused and looked over the crowd.

"But He is also just."

A ripple of fear went through the church. Everyone knew that God's invitation was generous, but they also knew that if they rejected God's goodness, then they would meet His wrath.

When the pastor gave the altar call, everyone rushed forward.

True Love

God is love, but God is also just. This foundational belief of all Christian denominations portrays God as the Source of blessings and suffering. The accepted view of God's judgment puts stones in God's hands and warns us that God is about to start throwing. Yes, God gives us eternal life, but He also throws us into hell and eternal death. God is good until His mercy runs out, then He is unyielding. Christianity's dualistic view of God resembles the philosophy of yin and yang more than the teachings of Jesus. The problem with Christianity is that our traditional view of God creates an intense aura of fear. On the surface, God seems good, but when His mercy is rejected, He turns ugly. This distorted view of God has created more atheists and terrified more Christians than any other Satanic lie.

I grew up believing that God the Father was watching me, keeping a record of my good and bad deeds in a book in heaven. I knew that if I was good enough, I would be welcomed into Pearly Gates, but if I failed or didn't live up to my potential or got caught with unforgiven sins, then there was no hope for me. My belief in a good God/bad God cop scenario created a stressed out, super Christian who careened from being a self-righteous hypocrite to a dirty, defeated sinner. I tried so hard to keep it together, but my temper got worse, and my internal anxiety destroyed my peace and joy. My marriage was in danger, and I came to a point where I questioned if the whole Christian thing was worth it.

Then Jesus stepped in between me and the lies that were hurling stones at my soul. He gently bent down next to me and began to write truth in the sand of my heart.

Conversations with my dad, podcasts on my phone, and Christian books with a wild, new perspective felt like putting on a warm coat on a cold morning. This new view of God came slowly at times because I am stubborn and hard headed. But eventually I came to realize that the God I served was not the same God Jesus revealed. The god I served was more like the pagan god Zeus of the ancient Greeks with his lightning bolts and nasty temper than the God Jesus revealed by His life and death.

When I saw God's true character and how He ran His universe or treated sinners, I no longer felt naked and ashamed in front of God. The question wasn't if I was good enough for God, but was God good enough for me? Would I trust Him completely with my messy life? Jesus showed me that God would never abandon me, and the choice to walk away was mine. I realized that God loves me unconditionally and that He never uses force to control or manipulate me.

I finally met the Man squatting in the sand with a stick in His hand. He was writing down the lies I believed and the sins I committed, and I heard Jesus say, "I am not here to condemn you." The more time I spent with Jesus, the more lies and sins He wiped away. At last, I stopped being afraid of God.

While I have grown in the last few years, I am not perfect. Understanding the truth about God has not transformed me into a man who never cusses, slips into sin, or gets discouraged, but Jesus has elevated my perspective of who God is. I am a better man, because I serve a better God. This book wasn't written by a saint, but by an average man who has seen God in a new way and can't wait to share the good news. I don't need to be perfect, because He is. God is good, kind, and loving … always.

Is it time for you to step out of the shadows of fear and into the warm sunlight of God's love? Understanding the truth about God's character reveals a God who refuses to throw stones, but instead takes off His robe of righteousness and offers it to us. He is the Judge who lets us decide if we will cling to our flimsy sheet or take His hand and slip into His warm cloak.

When we trust God's true character, accept His forgiveness, and put on His robe, we change. Jesus meets us where we are, bleeding, naked, and ready to die, but then He saves us, rescues us, and heals us. That is salvation.

The Dream

Joseph tossed and turned. He loved his fiance, but she was pregnant. He knew he couldn't marry her now, but he wanted to protect her as best he could.

He sighed and thought, *I'll divorce her quietly.* Then Joseph rolled over and fell into troubled dreams.

Suddenly a voice woke him. Joseph opened his eyes and gasped. An angel of light stood at the foot of his bed. His glory was so bright and his presence so strong, that Joseph shook in fear.

The angel raised its hand as if to calm Joseph and said, "Do not be afraid to take Mary as your wife, for the child conceived in her is of the Holy Spirit."

Joseph blinked and rubbed his eyes. *Am I dreaming?* he wondered.

The angel smiled. "She will bear a son, and you will call Him Jesus, for He will save His people from their sins." Then the angel vanished.

Joseph sat bolt upright in his bed. The room was dark, and he was alone, yet he could still hear the angel's voice.

"He will save His people from their sins."

Joseph put his hand on his beating heart. *The Messiah is coming!*[4]

---

4   Matthew 1:18-25

Sozo

When the angel spoke to Joseph, it promised that Jesus would *sozo* His people from their sins. This word in Greek has multiple meanings. While "to save" is the most common translation, the word also means "to heal" or "to rescue."[5] The angel was crystal clear. Jesus would save or heal or rescue us from *sin*.

The traditional view of salvation, the one I grew up with, said that Jesus came to die for our sins and save us from *punishment*. This punishment is doled out by God the Father after Judgment Day for everyone who is not covered by the blood of Christ. While this version of salvation had elements of truth, it blamed God for the pain of punishment instead of sin. When I believed this was true, I was afraid of God. This false salvation claimed to save me from God's righteous anger instead of sin's natural results.

At Golgotha, Jesus proved that sin is responsible for death, not God. On the cross, the Father let go of Jesus, and His Son called out, "My God, My God, why have You abandoned Me?"[6] His cry confirmed the fatal result of sin—separation from God, the Source of Life, which naturally leads to death.

Sin is a fatal disease that separates us from God. Jesus came to earth to *save* us from sin, to *rescue* us from its deadly poison, to *heal* our hearts, and to

---

5   https://biblehub.com/greek/4982.htm

6   Matthew 27:46

reconnect us to God. True salvation does so much more than take away our punishments for sin. It transforms our characters and wins our trust back to God. When I finally understood this view of salvation, I was drawn to God and wanted to be as close to Him as possible. Instead of running away from God and hiding, I ran to God.

This book highlights different attributes of God's character. Each one counters the currents of tradition and accepted theology, but each truth has broken a chain of bondage in my life and helped me trust God more. As you read this book, pray for wisdom. Let the Holy Spirit guide you and lead you into the truth that you need. I don't have all the answers, but I will point you to the One who does.

He's sitting at a table, surrounded by friends. The cross is only days away, and Mary wants to say thank you.

No Regrets

Mary slipped into the room. No one noticed her. The guests leaned against the table and talked as they munched on fresh figs and flatbread. Her bright eyes quickly took in the room. Her brother sat next to Jesus, drinking in every word the Teacher spoke. Simon, the host and a wealthy Pharisee, called a servant over to him and gave her orders. Jesus, holding a cup in one hand and gesturing with the other, launched into another story. A smile danced across His face, but Mary's heart was heavy. Jesus was going to die soon.

She knew this because just the other day Jesus was walking through a field with His followers, and after explaining a parable about seeds, a shadow fell across His face. Mary noticed it immediately.

"In Jerusalem I will suffer many horrible things." Jesus stopped absentmindedly picking a grain stalk as He stared over the fields. Jesus sighed. "When we get to Jerusalem, the priests and leaders will arrest me, condemn me, and then crucify me, but on the third day I will rise again."

Jesus' words felt like a kick in her gut. Mary's mind panicked. *Jesus Arrested!? Condemned!? Crucified!?* She struggled to understand Jesus' words. *How could this really happen?* She couldn't believe it. Mary missed the rest of the conversation lost in her thoughts. She knew that Jesus always spoke truth, and she wanted to do something before He died to show Him how much she loved Him. *What can I do for Jesus?* she wondered.

Suddenly Mary remembered the last funeral she'd attended. It had been her brother's. She remembered looking down on Lazarus' cold, lifeless body and being filled with regrets, so many regrets. There were words Mary wished she had spoken, jokes she wished she had shared, walks in the countryside she wished they had taken together, but Lazarus was dead, and the guilt of everything left undone only intensified her grief.

Then Mary smiled, remembering Jesus' words near Lazarus' tomb.

"Mary, I am the Resurrection and the Life. Those who believe in Me will never perish eternally." Then Jesus faced the open tomb. His strong voice shattered the darkness of death, "Lazarus! Come out!"

Mary shook her head, remembering the overwhelming joy she felt as her brother staggered out of the tomb. She had rushed to embrace Lazarus and promised herself that she would never wait for another funeral before telling the people she loved how much they meant to her. No more regrets. Not ever again. But what could she do for Jesus? Mary imagined Him lying in the cold tomb, like Lazarus. The thought brought tears to her eyes.

Then she had an idea.

The Perfume

It's time, Mary thought as she walked toward Jesus. He was leaning against the table with His elbow resting on a soft pillow. Without anyone seeing her, Mary quietly knelt at Jesus' feet and pulled the delicate stone jar of expensive perfume out from the folds of her robe. Her slender fingers snapped the bottle's long neck off quickly. Immediately a rich aroma filled the room.

The powerful scent reminded Mary of preparing her own brother's body for burial. Intense emotions welled up and spilled out in quiet tears. She couldn't imagine life without Jesus. Mary remembered the day Jesus had saved her from certain death. Jesus had looked into her sinful soul and loved her unconditionally. He had not condemned her but instead offered her His cloak and a whole new way of living. He had set her free.

Mary refocused on her task and slowly dribbled the sweet smelling perfume across His feet. Overcome with gratitude, she pulled down her long, brown hair and used it to spread the liquid. Tears dripped down her nose and fell onto Jesus' dirty feet. Mary noticed that no servant had washed them, and mud from the streets clung to His toes. She could smell the worn leather of His sandals and the dirt of the road mingling with the perfume. Gently Mary cleaned off the dirt with her tears and then dried His feet with her hair. Overcome with emotion, Mary bent over and kissed the feet of the Messiah, her Healer, her Savior.

She was so focused on her pain at the thought of losing Him, that Mary didn't notice the sudden silence in the room.

Someone loudly cleared his throat, and Mary looked up. Everyone was staring at her. Judas leaned over and grumbled something about wasteful extravagance and the needs of the poor. Mary's cheeks flushed with embarrassment. She hadn't meant for anyone to even notice her. She only wanted to honor Jesus while He was still alive.

Simon the Pharisee sniffed and raised his chin. Mary's eyes shot in his direction and quickly glanced away in shame. Simon knew far too many of her secrets.

I am so stupid! What was I thinking? This was a terrible idea! Accusing voices crashed around in Mary's head. *I should have known better.* Mary's tears obscured her vision as she fumbled for the bottle of ointment and rose to flee into the darkness outside. But Jesus' strong, calm voice stopped her.

"Simon," Jesus said, looking at His host. "I want to tell you a story." Then Jesus glanced at Mary reassuringly, nodding slightly for her to sit back down. His gentle eyes gave Mary courage. She sat down, safely placing herself just behind Jesus. Then she listened to His story about two servants who owed their master money. When Jesus finished the story, He placed a reassuring hand on Mary's shoulder.

"Look at this woman sitting beside me. Simon, when I entered your home, you didn't offer me water to wash the dust off my feet, but she has washed my feet with her tears and wiped them with her hair. You didn't greet me with a kiss, but she has kissed my feet." Jesus paused and inhaled deeply, clearly enjoying the wonderful fragrance that graced the room. "Simon, you didn't offer to anoint my head with olive oil, but she anointed my feet with a rare perfume."

Jesus smiled at the men sitting around the table and said, "This woman needed a whole lot of forgiveness, and she has shown me a whole lot of love. But the person who doesn't need a lot of forgiveness, doesn't show a lot of love."

Some of the men around the table continued to grumble, but Jesus ignored them and looked directly at Mary.

"Thank you," He said kindly. "Mary, your faith has saved you. You will live in peace."

Mary never forgot that moment. The strong scent of the perfume, the soft glow of the lamps, and the look of gratitude and love in Jesus' face were etched into her memory forever. There were many things Mary didn't understand, but there was one thing she knew. Jesus had rescued her, healed her, and now He was transforming her into a new woman through His constant love and grace.

Mary smiled. Jesus knew she loved Him wholeheartedly and trusted Him implicitly. Now, she had no regrets.[7]

Main Points: I am fearless because ...
God is good.
God is not here to judge me.
God is here to save me.
God is with me.

---

7   Luke 7:36-50

Chapter 2

THE LEADER

"Don't panic. I'm with you.
There's no need to fear for I'm
your God. I'll give you strength.
I'll help you. I'll hold you steady,
keep a firm grip on you."[8]
—God

The Cloud

They were trapped. Large, imposing mountains
loomed on either side of the beach while the sea
stretched out ahead of them for miles. Behind them,
a giant cloud of dust kicked up into the blue desert
sky. Joshua squinted against the setting sun and saw
flashes of bright metal and heard the harsh snaps

---

8   Isaiah 41:10 The Message

of whips as the Egyptian chariots charged down the narrow pass leading to the sea.

Joshua rushed up to Moses, "I can organize a defense!" he volunteered. "I'm sure some of the men in the camp have weapons. We will fight and hold the Egyptian army off as long as possible, while you lead our people to safety."

Moses smiled at his young assistant. Joshua was breathless and brave, but unaware of how futile his plans were. "God has led us to this place. I'm sure He will take care of us here," Moses said as he looked down on the multicolored tents pitched next to the Red Sea. He could see panicked faces and hear cries of despair mingled with shouts of rage rising from the makeshift camp. A group of tribal leaders stomped up the hill toward him and his young aide.

"Moses!" a man shouted. "I told you something like this would happen."

"Here comes Eliab," Joshua groaned. "I wish we had left him in Egypt."

Moses placed a calm hand on Joshua's shoulder. "Don't worry, young friend. God will fight this battle for us."

Eliab, who was the leader of the clan of Zebulun, marched directly up to Moses and poked the prophet hard in the chest with an accusing finger.

"Why did you bring us out here to be slaughtered by Pharaoh?" Eliab's angry red face was mere inches away from Moses. "Weren't there enough graves back in Egypt!?"

The mob behind Eliab shouted their approval, and a few men picked up stones and menacingly stepped toward Moses. Joshua edged forward to meet the angry crowd and defend his mentor, but the leader held out his hand for Joshua to stand down.

Eliab wasn't done. He furiously pointed to the chariots of Pharaoh's army swiftly drawing closer. "It would have been better for us to die as slaves in Egypt than to become corpses by the sea! Why did you make us leave, Moses? Why did you make us leave the safety of our homes?"

Moses ignored Eliab and turned toward the multitude. Most of the camp had come to stand before Moses. They looked to their leader for hope and courage. Moses read the terror in their upturned faces.

"Don't be afraid!" Moses said, calmly raising his hands over the people. "Stand firm, and you will see the deliverance of the Lord." The leader fearlessly faced the oncoming Egyptian army. The speeding chariots were almost within bowshot range. Joshua could see the famed archers holding their bows, ready to let the first wave of arrows fly.

"Today is the last day you will ever see the Egyptians," Moses promised. He looked up at the holy cloud towering above them. Its shade had led the Hebrews out of Egypt, protected them from the scorching sun, and had comforted them with the promise of God's constant presence. Moses smiled, "The Lord will fight for you. You need only to be still."

Joshua nodded and took a deep, calming breath. The young warrior looked down at the shovel in his hand. "God will fight for me," Joshua repeated. Then he tossed the makeshift weapon to the ground and grinned. *This is going to be good.* He looked at Moses standing before the people.

The old man's gray head was bowed in prayer, and his lips moved quietly. Joshua reverently bowed his head too, quietly thanking the Lord for the promised deliverance and repeated, "The Lord will fight for you. You need only to be still," over and over to himself. Each time he said the phrase, the cold fear in his heart thawed until it was completely gone, replaced by a warm feeling of peace and hope. Joshua felt the sea breeze brush his face. It was gentle and carried a faint hint of jasmine. Joshua took a deep breath and thought of the Promised Land. He opened his eyes. "Be still," he said calmly.

Then the ground shook and rumbled as thousands of horse hooves pounded the desert floor. The familiar cracks of the Egyptian whips sounded close. Joshua lifted his head and glared at the oncoming army.

The Egyptian horde was magnificent. Their armor glinted with gold, and their war stallions were the envy of every monarch in the east. This cruel army knew only victory, and their confidence showed. Joshua understood their objective for his people: rape, slaughter, and a merciless return to slavery.

Suddenly the wind rose and the tents flapped and snapped as the immense cloud growled and lumbered toward the Egyptians. Joshua looked up. The Lord was beginning to fight for His people.

Most of the Hebrews missed the movement in the sky and instead chose to stare at the oncoming host of chariots. The army was close, very close.

Just then the Hebrews heard the shrill cry of the Egyptian trumpets, and immediately a thousand arrows darkened the desert sky, their shafts arching upward, catching the last rays of the red sun and streaking like falling stars across the dark blue sky. Mesmerized, a million eyes watched as death flew through the sky, beautiful yet sinister. The arrows reached their peak and then tilted ominously downwards, plunging toward the terrified Hebrews. Joshua watched the wall of doom careening directly toward him and refused to blink at the sharp whistle of arrows slicing the air. Instinctively, he raised his arm to shield his face, but Joshua stood firm, trusting God's deliverance.

"You need only to be still," he muttered defiantly.

Suddenly, a rush of wind blew past Joshua, almost knocking him over. God's holy cloud surged directly into the path of the oncoming arrows. The wind screamed past Joshua, whipping his short tunic and kicking sand up into the air, and the arrows disappeared into the thick cloud.

Then above the wind, he heard clinks and clatters. Blown off course, the arrows tumbled and flipped through the air, crashing to the ground, they bounced and snapped on the hard desert rocks. Falling like rain before the camp, the harmless arrows soon covered the ground in broken piles. Not one arrow found its mark. The cloud had stopped every single one.

Amazed, Joshua dropped to his knees and lifted his hands in awe. Prayer and praise flowed from him as the wind continued to howl. The billowing cloud stalked menacingly toward the Egyptian army. Joshua watched as the troops and charioteers skidded to a halt and sheer panic broke out of their ranks. Soldiers leaped from their chariots, threw down their weapons, and cried out in terror.

The cloud formed a massive barricade between the Egyptians and the Hebrews and threw a pall of darkness over the cowering warriors. It settled onto the ground with a mighty rumble, filling up the pass and blocking the Egyptian's route to the beach and God's people. The angel of the Lord, which had gone before the people in the cloud, now moved to protect their camp. The Hebrews were still trapped, but they were safe for now.

Joshua turned back toward Moses, surprised to see the older man's head still bent in prayer. Joshua knew he should wait, but he couldn't contain his excitement any longer. He dashed up to his mentor and eagerly tugged on Moses' sleeve.

"Moses!" Joshua exclaimed beaming. "Did you see that!? The clouds and the wind and the arrows! It's … it's … it's so …" Joshua couldn't find the right word, but he didn't care.

Moses chuckled and opened his eyes. "I told you, God would fight for us." Then Moses stood to his feet and gazed over the vast sea. The wind now whipped the waves into whitecaps, and the thunder of their surging crashes echoed against the mountain walls. Moses leaned closer to Joshua and winked. "You haven't seen anything yet."

Then Moses walked up the mountainside toward a large rock overlooking the sea. His steps were confident and purposeful, like God was about to do something great. Joshua started to follow Moses, but then he paused. A still, small voice beckoned him to stay back, to wait. This moment was not for him.

The desert sky was gray with the last streaks of sunlight slipping beyond the horizon. Joshua turned back to camp and looked toward the cloud. He gasped. Now the cloud glowed and vibrated with an intense holy energy, lighting up the night with its bright, orange fire. The dusky sky slipped into the black of night while the sea disappeared into the gloom, but the brilliance from the cloud lit the camp as if the sun still shone. Joshua shook his head awestruck.

"Dear God, I will always remember this night, and I'll never doubt your goodness again," Joshua promised. Smiling, the young man looked back at Moses.

The prophet stood on the rocky outcropping holding his staff, his back to the bright camp and his face to the dark sea. Joshua knew Moses was still praying. Joshua watched Moses lift his staff over his head and hold it high with both hands.

Joshua held his breath, waiting. The wind shifted. At first, the change was so slight Joshua hardly noticed, but soon the wind grew in strength. The fiery cloud remained lodged between the freed slaves and their former masters, but the howling wind no longer blew toward the desert. Now it rushed toward the sea, gaining in strength and fury.

Joshua shielded his eyes with a hand and squinted through the wind at the shore. The waves no longer crashed onto the beach, instead they fled toward deeper water. The beach was growing, reaching out into the sea, stretching into the depths as the water raged and piled into giant swells slowly rolling back in opposite directions. Joshua heard the woosh of the wind as the gale intensified and drove even deeper into the water. Frothy waves tumbled back from the wind's violent fury, and soon two giant walls of white water stood guard over a path straight through the middle of the sea. Joshua's mouth dropped open in astonishment.

Moses walked quickly back down from the rock and spoke to Joshua. "We must get the people ready," the prophet said. "We need to … " But Moses stopped suddenly when he saw the look on Joshua's face. The older man smiled and looked at the road emerging in the middle of the dark sea.

"God is amazing, isn't He?" he said softly. "Remember this day, my son. Our journey to the Promised Land holds many obstacles, but our God will deliver us." Moses placed his hand on Joshua's shoulder. "Remember this day." Then he turned and quickly marched into the camp, barking orders and getting the people ready to move.

Dry Ground

By the time the Hebrews were ready to move, the sea floor was completely dry. Moses stood at the edge of the sea and spoke to the people. His strong voice thundered over the vast throng.

"People of Israel," Moses began. "The Lord our God has heard your cries for deliverance, and you have witnessed His mighty power."

The prophet pointed to the path slicing through the tall, dark waters. "Our only hope is to trust in God and walk through the sea. If anyone stays on this beach, the Egyptians will kill them. This is the only way. Trust in God's goodness and take it." Moses took a few steps towards the waves. He paused and smiled. "Follow me," he said.

Then Moses strode down into the sea. Strong emotions washed over Joshua. Moses' words spoke directly to his heart.

"I want to be a leader like that," Joshua said in awe. Then he smiled and trotted to catch up to Moses.

When he reached Moses, Joshua looked up at the water towering on either side of the dry ground. "Did you know God would do this?" Joshua asked.

Moses looked at his young friend and grinned. "I had no idea what God was going to do." The two men chuckled, and then Moses turned serious and looked deeply into Joshua's eyes. "But I had no doubt that God would deliver us."

Moses slapped Joshua on the back. "This is going to be one epic journey," he said.

Joshua nodded. He looked over his shoulder and saw thousands of people streaming off the beach and down onto the dry sea floor. He peered up past the lofty walls of water to the sliver of sky overhead.

"The Lord will fight for you." Joshua said reverently. "You need only to be still."[9]

God's Leadership Style

As we listen to the rushing winds and hear the crash of the storm tossed Red Sea, we catch a glimpse of God's leadership style. The Almighty God of the Universe used His power to guide and protect. The cloud of shade, the fire lighting up the camp, and

---

9   Exodus 14 NLT

the path through the sea are all examples of God's leadership. Many people in the world today misunderstand God's power and instead see dominating force. They examine God's laws and see random tests of obedience. When these misrepresentations burrow deep into the mind, they breed rebellion and fear. Salvation is built on faith, and to be saved, we must see the truth about God's leadership and His laws.

The Two Kings

Over two thousand years ago, in a land far away, there lived two kings. These two kings couldn't have been more different. The king of Persia was wildly rich while the other king led the simple city state of Sparta. The Persian monarch had more wives than the stars in the heavens while the Spartan king had grown old with one faithful woman. Xerxes, the ruler of Persia, was young and brash while Leonidas, the leader of the Spartans, was old and thoughtful. Yet the most distinct difference between these two monarchs was their relationship with their men. Xerxes was willing to sacrifice many men in his thirst of conquest, while Leonidas was willing to sacrifice his own life for his soldiers and his subjects. Xerxes sat in opulence, drinking rare wine in golden goblets, watching his soldiers fight from the safety of his massive throne, but Leonidas faced down the enemy, shoulder to shoulder with his comrades. When these two kings met, Xerxes won the battle but lost the war and drifted into the oblivion of history. Leonidas died alongside his men, cut down by a Persian blade. In death, the rugged king of Sparta achieved the dream of every Greek warrior—immortality won on the fields of war.

The Battle of Thermopylae lasted only a few days. Three hundred Spartans led by their old king, Leonidas, held the narrow mountain pass against countless waves of invading Persian soldiers. Xerxes, the ruler of Persia with lands stretching from Egypt to India, thought crushing the independent city-states of Greece would be easy, but he didn't count on meeting men like King Leonidas and his Spartan warriors. They fought with a calm fury and faced death with indifference. Although the Spartan soldiers were outnumbered, ill-equipped, surrounded by overwhelming forces, and facing certain death, they fought with confidence and discipline. After a few clashes, the Spartan's red cloaks and long hair terrified Xerxes' men. When the Persian trumpets sounded, the Persian soldiers refused to march forward. Enraged, Xerxes ordered men to drive his soldiers forward with whips into the bristling shield wall of Sparta.

Xerxes watched the engagement from a hill and marveled at the Spartan soldiers. He sent men to capture other Greeks so he could question them about these terrible warriors. Xerxes learned of the soldiers' lifelong commitment to war, of their harsh training schools, and of their kings. He learned about the Agoge, the school where Spartan monarchs went through the same brutal military training as the other boys. Future kings of Sparta wrestled in the sand with commoners and stood in the shield line where the fighting was the thickest.

Then Xerxes learned of the prophecy from Delphi. It proclaimed tragedy for Sparta. The prophetess had declared Sparta would lose either their noble king or their beloved city. For Leonidas, the choice was simple. He marched into battle knowing he would die but believing that his death would ultimately save his people. King Xerxes could not fathom this self-sacrifice, yet he could not deny its impact on the men of Sparta, for they fought like lions.

On the last day of the battle, King Leonidas fell, struck by one of Xerxes' men. The Persian invaders grabbed his body and hauled it back to their lines, but seeing this, the Spartan warriors surged forward in reckless abandon. They clawed, bit, and tore their way to the bloody remains of their king. They rescued his body and gently carried it back to their own lines.

Xerxes gasped in disbelief. Why would men risk their lives to save a corpse? The little Spartan band of soldiers now stood on the crest of a small hill, armed with daggers, broken spears, and a few swords. Their armor shattered, their numbers few, their king slain, yet they stood and fought until the last brave warrior lay dead.

Xerxes later walked through the battlefield, slowly moving past hundreds of his own lifeless soldiers. When he came to the small hill, he began to step over fallen Spartans who looked no different than his men. In fact, they were physically smaller than many of his warriors. In death, the Spartans had lost their invincible aura. Then Xerxes came to the body of King Leonidas. Xerxes saw that the king was old and gray. He saw that his armor and clothing was the same as his men. The victorious monarch shook his head at the foolishness of the Greeks. Kings were supposed to be feared, not loved. Kings were supposed to be served, not to serve. Subjects and soldiers were supposed to die for their kings. Kings should never die for their people. Xerxes stepped over the fallen king in disgust and stalked off the field.

Leonidas and his brave three hundred soldiers slowed the Persian advance long enough to give the Greeks time to unite. Even though the Persian invaders burned Athens, the next battle ended very differently. After his humiliating naval defeat in the waters off Salamis, Xerxes returned to his empire, leaving a general to conquer the city-states of Greece. On the plains of Plataea, the entire army of Sparta with all the men of Greece marched out to avenge Leonidas and his men. The Persians suffered a catastrophic defeat and never threatened the land of Greece again. Many historians believe that Leonidas and his men saved democracy at Thermopylae. One king sacrificed his life and gave a voice to the lives of millions who would follow after him. This is true leadership.

Dominance Leadership

There are two types of leaders, and they are polar opposites. The Dominance leaders rule through force and fear, while Influence leaders use freedom and love.[10] Reaching all the way back to before the fall of the Roman Empire, Christian tradition placed God in the wrong category. Concepts that crept into the Christian faith like purgatory and penance gave God Dominance leadership traits. Now many modern Christians are unaware that they still see God through the lens of Dominance leadership. Every spiritual truth, every command, even every promise is filtered through that dark lens. Unfortunately, if we use the wrong filter, we fail to see the truth about God. Then we miss out on all the peace and power of Christianity and slip into an existence of fear and doubt.

---

10   The two theories of leadership: Dominance and Influence have been modified from the original theories of Maner and Case, who classified all leaders under the categories of Dominance and Prestige.

Maner, J. K., & Case, C. R. (2016). *Dominance and prestige: Dual strategies for navigating social hierarchies*. Advances in Experimental Social Psychology.

Leader

Everyone Else

The best way to understand Dominance leadership is to think of a pyramid. The top block, the pinnacle, represents the leader. This is the highest position with the most honor. All stones of the entire building support the leader. Energy flows up the pyramid for the benefit of the leader.

Historically, Dominance is the most common leadership style. The Pharaohs, the Caesars, even the dictators of modern day ruled through the principles of Dominance leadership. Machiavelli, in his masterpiece work on leadership *The Prince*, fully supported Dominance philosophy when he argued that the end justifies the means. When leaders believe that they are free to take any means necessary to make their goals a reality, innocent people always suffer. These ruthless leaders see themselves as the apex block and will use every other stone in the pyramid to accomplish their goals and build up their legacy.

This Dominance style corrupts common men, transforming them into monsters who justify the use of force and threaten anyone who stands in their way. They cheat and lie and send henchmen to arrest, torture, and kill their opponents. They rule through the power of fear. Many leaders have risen to glorious heights using these tactics, but no one followed them out of devotion or loyalty. The minions obeyed and cheered and bowed only because they were afraid of punishment and retribution.

Caesar Augustus

A classic example of this type of leadership emerges in the life of Caesar Augustus. This man was a political genius. He befriended enemies by killing his old friends. He stole vast amounts of wealth through trickery and entrapment. He invaded countries and toppled dynasties. He pleased the people by calling himself *Princep*, First Citizen, yet he ruled the Roman Senate with the authority of a tyrant king. He brought peace to the world and began the *Pax Romana*, a two-hundred year stretch of peace and prosperity while his secret police kidnapped, tortured, and assassinated anyone who threatened his power. He demanded loyalty and respect. Augustus could elevate any man to glorious heights or make him disappear forever. This Caesar was the classic manipulator, playing men against each other. He had a knack for knowing when to be kind or when to kill. While his political life was monumentally successful, he did not inspire devotion from those closest to him. Augustus, a cold, distant leader, reached the heights of world domination through the calculated strategies of Dominance leadership.[11]

Influence Leadership

Everyone Else

Leader

On the other side of the spectrum, Influence leadership shines as a bright contrast. Imagine that same pyramid, but this time flip it upside down so that it balances on its point. Now instead of the pyramid supporting the leader, the leader actually supports the entire pyramid. The Influence leader sends energy up through the structure to empower every single individual. Such leaders are extremely rare historically. Influence leaders do not believe the end justifies the means especially when it justifies cruelty or selfishness. These leaders share their vision and then leave others free to follow or reject their authority. As demonstrated in the upside down pyramid, these leaders suffer immense personal sacrifices for the good of their followers. Influence

---

11   Goldsworthy, Adrian Keith. *Augustus: First Emperor of Rome*. New Haven: Yale University Press, 2014.

leaders are the only leaders completely trustworthy because they never manipulate or coerce others. Their lasting legacy is not how high they personally went, but how high they lifted others up.

Influence leaders rarely resort to force, and when they do exercise their power, it disciplines, trains, or defends their followers. Instead of becoming monsters, Influence leaders fight monsters. They are dangerous, but only to the enemy. Their followers obey them out of respect, devotion, and love. Influence leaders can also reach glorious heights of fame and power, surrounded by adoring supporters. Their morals, their characters, and their dreams draw men and women into their influence more powerfully than any threats or punishments ever could. These are the best leaders the world has ever seen.

George Washington

George Washington was a tall, quiet man from Virginia. He was not a political or military genius. He actually lost more battles than he won, and he was a terrible public speaker. But George Washington had character, and he had a dream of what American could become. He truly believed in the ideals of the American Revolution, and one day his leadership single-handedly saved that dream.

The Battle of Monmouth erupted before General Washington could arrive. General Charles Lee led the Continental troops into battle hoping to gain a quick victory and steal the top spot in the Army from Washington, but the British quickly routed the Americans.[12]

Lee panicked and ordered a full retreat. Then he fled the field, leaving the men alone. As soon as Washington caught wind of the disaster, he rode to the front lines. On his way, he met Lee. The contrast was dramatic. Lee was flustered, full of fear and blame, and thinking only of his life and his legacy. Washington was steady, full of fury and courage, thinking only of the abandoned men and the cause he loved. Lee dashed away from the battle, and Washington rode directly into the thickest part of the fight.

Washington thundered onto the battlefield and reigned his mount in front of a group of retreating men. His eyes were ablaze, and he shouted, "Will you fight?"

The soldiers stopped running and looked up at their General. They remembered Valley Forge, where Washington had shivered in the cold with them. They remembered crossing the frozen Delaware, where he had led them to a dazzling victory. They knew Washington. They loved Washington. The soldiers lifted their muskets and gave him three hearty cheers. Then they spun to face the British bayonets.

---

12   Chernow, Ron. *Washington: A Life*. London: Allen Lane, 2010.

General Lafayette, a French volunteer and life-long admirer of Washington, wrote, "His presence stopped the retreat. I thought then as now that I never beheld so superb a man."[13]

Washington rode all across the battlefield that hot day. He encouraged, scolded, and led the men from the front until his majestic white warhorse fell dead underneath him from exhaustion. He calmly mounted another and continued to lead. His powerful presence inspired the men more than his mediocre tactical decisions. They followed a man they loved. What started as an American retreat resulted in a British defeat. While strategically inconclusive, the battle sealed Washington in his role as the commander-in-chief and paved the way for his later presidency.

Caesar Augustus and George Washington are renowned men of history who capture the essence of the two leadership styles. Augustus briefly ruled the world, while Washington continues to inspire and influence to this day. Caesar forced millions to do his bidding, while George Washington inspired millions to think as free men and act with integrity. Augustus was feared, while Washington is still admired as one of American's greatest founding fathers.

---

13   Flexner, James. *George Washington in the American Revolution, 1775-1783 (Boston: Little, Brown, 1968), 305.*

God's Leadership

World history holds many examples of Dominance and Influence leadership, but let's look at the spiritual realm and examine God's leadership style. After reading parts of the Old Testament, many jump to the conclusion that God is a Dominance leader. Doesn't God threaten, punish, and even kill? When we look closer, we see a pattern that points to a different leadership style. To truly understand the big picture, we must go to the beginning.

Before planet Earth was created, the mighty angel Lucifer stood closest to God's throne. He possessed more gifts than any other creature, yet his heart turned greedy and he wanted more. He looked at God with jealousy. Sin grew like a poisonous weed in his heart, transforming him from Lucifer the Light Bearer, into Satan, the accusing Deceiver. Since Satan knew he could not defeat God by force, for God was all-powerful, Satan spread lies about God in heaven and then came to earth to continue his quest to kill trust in the Almighty.

Satan's most successful tactic was to take his own evil, self-seeking characteristics and stick them on God. The first lie of the Universe was that God was a Dominance leader. Satan told the angels that God was cruel, controlling, and could not be trusted. Revelation tells us of a war in heaven. The Greek word used for *war* is *polemos*.[14] This is where we get the

---

14   https://biblehub.com/greek/4171.htm

English word *polemic*, which means a harsh verbal or written attack. When Revelation describes a *polemos* in heaven, it means debate or argument, obviously not actual physical fight between an All-Powerful God and angels. The Deceiver used freedom that automatically comes with love to spread fear and distrust in God. Satan told lies, and God gave opposing evidence. Finally, after all the arguments and evidence, every angel made a decision. Satan with one third of the angels chose to continue to fight against God, because they could no longer tolerate God's loving presence.

Creation

In the midst of this war, God spoke. His Word created the heavens and the earth. Intelligent beings witnessed God's awesome power as He formed the sun, the oceans, and animals with mere words. The book of Job says that at creation the sons of God sang for joy.[15] Our world emerged in the middle of a conflict between good and evil with intelligent beings watching God's every move. The heavenly debate centered on God's true character, and God created the world as prime evidence of His true nature. He displayed immense power for six days and then let the Universe examine His work on the seventh day.

God pointed to a world teeming with other-centered giving where every living thing from the giant

---

15   Job 38:7

redwood trees to the delicate water lily, from the smallest hummingbird to the largest blue whale, operated in harmony with the laws of selfless love. No creature lived selfishly, and it was good.

Then God formed man and woman in the ultimate example of how selfless love creates life. Adam was to give Eve his strength, and Eve was to give Adam her tenderness. Together they would create new life and selflessly pour their love into their children. The planet would pulse with the flow of love, and the Universe could understand God's true character and choose once again to trust in Him.

Satan saw an opportunity. If he could twist humanity's trust into fear, then he could blame God for all the pain and suffering that would naturally follow.

The Garden

Adam and Eve's favorite part of the day was when the Designer arrived and walked with them through the garden. Being in God's presence recharged their hearts and minds. He taught them about the plants and the animals, about the skies and the stars. He showed the new couple the natural laws that governed their new world. God smiled as He answered their eager questions and told them fascinating stories. He listened as they excitedly talked about their hopes and dreams. Many times God threw back His head and laughed as He walked with an arm around

Adam and Eve's shoulders. The new couple always felt safe and accepted in God's presence. The warm glow of His smile and the way He tilted His head to the side when He listened drew their hearts to His. God gently touched the flowers as He showed Eve the best way to care for them, and He helped Adam build a trellis for the vegetables as He explained the best way to care for Eve. Sometimes all three sat in the shade of a giant tree or dipped their feet into the cool stream as they watched the sunset.

Every evening when God arrived in the garden, He called out, "Adam. Eve. Where are you?" God knew where they were, but He waited for an invitation. The couple was always happy to see God. They would come running or call for Him to join them to swim in the lagoon or set out a feast of the freshest vegetables straight from Eve's garden. God was always welcome in their home.

One evening as the sun dipped behind the hills, the Designer told them about the war in heaven and how selfishness destroyed the peace and joy of His home. He pointed to the Tree of Knowledge and warned the couple that if they let selfishness into their hearts, then it would kill them. He was silent for a long time. Eve saw tears in God's eyes. She reached out and touched His arm. He looked deeply into her eyes and said, "I will love you forever." She smiled and leaned her head on His shoulder. God put His hand on Adam's arm and repeated His promise. "I will love you forever." The three sat in silence for a long time that evening.

The Fall

Then it happened. Adam and Eve ate the fruit, and everything changed.

That evening when God called out, no one answered. The Designer wasn't welcome in the garden this night. God knew what had happened, and His heart was broken. The friends God had formed with His own hands had walked away. Adam and Eve trusted a talking snake instead of their Creator. They had chosen selfishness, and it had already started to kill them. God had warned them about the dangers of distrust, but they believed Satan's lies about God's character. The snake told them God was selfish and holding them back from their full potential. It hissed that distrust and disobedience would transform them into wise and powerful gods.

Adam and Eve swallowed Satan's lies and his fruit. Immediately, the man and woman shivered with shame. They both hung their heads and averted their eyes. For the first time, they noticed the soft glow of light that covered their bodies had vanished. The biting wind felt chilly. Bitter and ashamed, they turned away from each other. They were naked, and it was not good.

Adam frantically grabbed some fig leaves and sewed them together to make coverings for himself and his wife. Eve was crying, and Adam was angry. They were both terrified. What would God do? Would He kill them on the spot? They had separated themselves from God's love and already doubted His goodness.

Then evening came, and they heard His voice. Adam's heart pounded, and he broke out into a cold sweat. Panic choked Eve's throat, and her palms felt clammy. They both ducked behind some bushes and felt sick to their stomachs. In the past, God's loving, gentle voice always sparked joy, but now it filled them with dread. Their breathing was quick and shallow, and their vision blurred.

Even though the couple was ashamed and afraid, God kept calling. His voice cracked, and Eve thought the Designer was crying. Finally Adam couldn't take it any longer. With his head hung in shame, he stepped out from behind the bushes and whispered, "Here I am."

God walked toward Adam, but the man kept his eyes on the ground. Eve crept up behind Adam. They heard God's footsteps coming closer. Adam took a deep breath and braced himself, and Eve closed her eyes. What would God do? Would He yell? Would He hurt them?

Then they were in His arms. God pulled Adam close and kissed Eve's forehead. They melted into Him and sobbed. Tears slid down God's cheeks as He held them for a long time. He cried for Adam and Eve. He cried for their children. He cried as

He saw all the pain and misery that their choice would bring.

The Lamb

Later all three stood next to an altar. Adam held a bloody flint knife in his hand. Eve watched in horror as the life slowly ebbed out of the little lamb.

So this is sin, she thought. *This is death.* She shuddered and leaned her head on Adam's shoulder.

Then the man and the woman looked at God. A tear slid down His cheek, and He pointed to the knife. "Sin is like that knife. It severs life, bringing death. Sin separates and destroys. Now that sin has entered your world, life will be different."

He looked at Adam. "The ground will be hard." Then He looked at Eve, "Childbirth and raising children will be painful."

Then He placed a hand on the quiet form of the lamb. "When you were connected to Me, you were connected to life. My energy, goodness, and love flowed through you just like the blood flowed through the lamb. But when you chose to separate yourselves from Me, you sliced through the artery that connected you to the Source of Life. This knife, which killed this little lamb, represents sin.."

"Sin will kill you," God said sadly. "Sin always brings pain. Sin always brings death."

Adam looked at the still lamb and then at his quivering hand. The awful truth began to dawn in his mind. *What have I done?* he wondered in anguish. This was the first time he had ever seen death. It was no longer abstract; death was real. Adam and Eve had thrown away intimacy with God for a fling with a snake who promised them enlightenment but instead delivered the poison of death. He held up the bloody knife and hated sin.

Then God gave Adam and Eve hope. "Even though we cannot be together in the same way, I will never leave you or forsake you," He said. "You won't be able to see Me, and many times you won't be able to feel my presence, but I AM still with you."

He stood next to the altar and spread out His arms. "One day I will come to take away the knife, to heal your wound and restore our connection. I will die like this lamb, but my death will give you life. Then you and all your children will have another chance to make another choice. You can pick up the knife of sin that will kill you or you can accept healing and live forever."

Eve gasped, and Adam swallowed hard. They did not understand. They expected God to be angry and punish them, but He had held them, cried with them, and now promised to die for them.

Adam shook his head and asked, "Why?"

God stood in front of Adam and placed a warm hand on his shoulder. Adam saw tears in God's eyes and felt the answer before he heard it. God swallowed hard and said, "I will love you forever."[16]

---

16   Genesis 3

The Battle Over the Promise

The war between good and evil centered on God's promise. God gave humanity the sacrificial system to show us how painful and destructive sin really is and to point us to the promised Savior. This system of worship captured the core value of Influence leadership: a leader selflessly giving to help others. It was another solid piece of evidence pointing to God's goodness, but slowly Satan twisted that truth. As pagan religions emerged, the sacrifices mutated from reminders of the Messiah to appeasing a divine, Dominance-style monster. The religions of the world sank into the hopeless worship of appeasement and fear. Humanity lost sight of God's promise and His goodness, and frantically tried to earn heaven's favor with costly sacrifices. Finally, even the Jews, the people blessed with more truth than any other nation, fell into the lie and saw God as a Dominance leader and sacrifice as the only way to appease His righteous wrath.

The Truth

From the humble beginning in a feeding trough to the epic end on the cross, Jesus fought the satanic lie that God was a Dominance leader. Instead of arriving as a prince pampered with pomp and prestige, Jesus was born to poor peasants and welcomed by smelly shepherds. Jesus and his parents spent years as refugees in Egypt, then moved to a town with a bad reputation where He worked with his hands in a carpenter's shop. Nothing Jesus did smacked of dominance. He wasn't physically intimidating or outwardly remarkable. He never used His divine power for show. Jesus was disappointingly normal. Instead of building an army or a reputation, Jesus was building His character, the foundation of every great Influence leader.

When the time was right, Jesus stepped out of normal and into greatness. He started His conquest by being baptized by a wildman in a muddy river. Then Jesus disappeared into the desert for forty days and defeated Satan's strongest temptations with simple Bible verses. Jesus showed up in small towns and simple weddings. He charged into the cosmic battle by talking to fishermen and teaching tax collectors. Even though Jesus was doing the exact opposite of what the people expected the coming Messiah to do, He had the audacity to burst into the public view and declare, "The Kingdom of Heaven is here!"

This announcement thrilled every Jewish heart. Visions of victory and glory filled their heads, but instead of giving the rally cry and calling for volunteers, instead of sending His countrymen into battle, Jesus called twelve average men to follow Him. Instead of rousing speeches, Jesus told stories about fields of wheat and lost coins. Instead of courting the rich and building alliances with the powerful,

Jesus healed sick children and encouraged the depressed. Jesus "wasted" His time with the bottom dwellers of society, healing them, teaching them, and helping them.

Sometimes Jesus did impressive things, like feeding the five thousand or raising the dead back to life, but Jesus never used His miracles to dominate, intimidate, or gain power for Himself. The flashes of greatness always benefited someone else.

The Jews, who saw God as a Dominance leader, imagined the Messiah appearing out of the desert with power and fury, but Jesus' presence and practices were baffling. For many Jews, their disappointment turned to hatred as they realized that Jesus would never fit the mold of the God they wanted.

But what if the Jews had expected an Influence leader? Then Jesus' actions and words would have made complete sense. The Baby of Bethlehem's stables, born at the bottom of the pyramid, grew into the Carpenter who built people up by healing them, blessing them, and teaching them. Everyone who accepted His touch and His words was changed forever.

Jesus told stories about mercy and faith, selfless love and hope, and then brought those stories into living color by His actions. Jesus focused on impacting individuals and didn't care about etiquette, social status, or the rules of engagement. That's why He spoke to the Samaritan woman at the well. That's why He called crusty sailors, crooked tax collectors, and passionate zealots to be His disciples. Jesus never forced anyone to obey him. He simply said, "Follow me," and kept walking. His ministry was devoid of manipulation or deception because it was simple, pure love. Jesus showed the world that instead of demanding sacrifice, God *became* the sacrifice and proved that God can be trusted, that He is love, that He is good. By going to the cross, Jesus showed that God will never manipulate, coerce, intimidate, or use force selfishly. These are as foreign to God's character as darkness is to light. When we see Jesus as an Influence leader, His entire ministry from the first sermon to His last breath on the cross is beautifully aligned.

Jesus' incredible sacrifice proved that God is good and nothing like the pagan gods who ruled the rest of the world. God's amazing grace was a message of hope and deliverance. Jesus' life and death was the final piece of evidence in God's defense. God is not a god of Dominance; He is an Influence leader.

Unfortunately, only a few people understood this truth, so Jesus gave His disciples the responsibility to share this good news, the Gospel, to the world.

Christianity Today

The old pagan lie thrives today. Many Christians still worship a god of Dominance and call him "Jesus" or "God the Father." Some pray to Mary or the saints because they fear God won't listen without intervention. Many Christians try to earn the Father's favor and stress over unconfessed sins, because they believe that He is more concerned with a list of legal requirements than with our characters. Preachers teach that Jesus bore the deadly wrath of God, that God's righteous anger killed His Son. They also preach that now God needs His Son to intercede on our behalf before He will show us mercy. We blame God for bad things that happen saying, "It was God's will." We believe God sends people to hell because they don't belong to the right church or have the right rituals. Mainstream Christianity portrays God as a punishing, judgmental, intolerant bully. Then we wonder why our churches are empty, why the gospel is repulsive to many, why we are living in fear.

The lie that God is a Dominance leader delights Satan. Most Christians don't believe it's a lie. All Christians say that God is good, but if we see God using Dominance principles, then our beliefs contradict our claims. This crack in our armor shows up when the battle turns ugly. We blame God, demand answers, and wonder why God didn't protect us. We don't enjoy calm peace in the storms of life. We turn to other sources to numb our pain. Christians suffer with depression, addiction, anxiety, and abuse. But if the gospel is powerless to change us, it is not the gospel. Any ideas that make us afraid of God, that make us doubt His goodness, that make us want to pull away from Him, come from Satan.

Jesus came to deliver us from lies about God. But He can save us only if we let Him. First, we must trust Him, for the righteous are saved by faith. This means that we must drop our fear of God and pick up our faith in Him. Jesus lived to calm our fears. His sermons, His miracles, and His death all shout the good news. God is trustworthy!

God's Laws

Our view of God's leadership directly impacts our beliefs about His laws. Dominance leaders impose rules, enforce them, and dole out punishments and rewards based on the performance of their followers. Influence leaders teach principles that lead to benefits to those who follow them. Far from being tests of obedience, these guidelines protect the faithful and guide them into harmony with reality. When we understand the true nature of God's laws, we see that their purpose is not to condemn us, but to help us heal.

Imposed Law

Satan's ultimate goal is to pull people away from trusting God, so he lies about God's leadership and His law. Satan's subtle lie is that God's law is Imposed Law. The deceiver portrays God as the great dictator in the sky, who rules with Dominance leadership. He says that God's law is the same as any other tyrant. Instead of seeing God as the Creator of the Universe, Satan succeeds in getting us to picture God as a despot imposing His will on us through arbitrary rules designed to enforce obedience.

When we see God as a Dominance leader using Imposed Law, we naturally pull away and stop trusting Him. We become convinced that God's rules exist to test the loyalty of His subjects. We are expected to obey in blind faith. Some of God's rules seem unscientific, out of date, or absurd, and because the underlying belief is that they are imposed by a divine dictator, many don't try to discover the purpose behind the principle. Many people think that God's rules and His judgments make Him look selfish. When punishments for disobedience seem arbitrary, grace and mercy come across as weak or unfair. It looks like God plays favorites with some people but enjoys punishing others. Satan's brilliant "theology" destroys faith in God and results in suffering. We sow self-destructive behavior and blame God when we reap a deadly harvest.

Natural Law

The truth is that God's law is Natural Law. He is the Creator, and His laws bring stability and order. If they are violated, pain is the natural result. Choices always have consequences. That's reality. God's natural laws, like gravity, are logical and universal. They protect us from chaos and death.

When we understand the nature of God's laws and obey them, the healing process begins. Instead of destroying ourselves through foolish, selfish behavior, we make choices that are in line with reality and result in positive outcomes and growth.

When Christians see God's laws as natural manifestations of the Universe, then everything changes for the better. We see His laws created for our benefit, holding the keys to health, social harmony, and inner peace. We see that God's goal is our growth and maturity, not shallow outward compliance. We begin to build our trust in God as we see the results. When we realize that following God's way works, a light bulb turns on. Sin loses its power on us, not because we are afraid of God, but because we are afraid of sin. We see sin as poison and refuse to drink it. Trust in God's instructions creates a better life.

Often God's laws are portrayed as a tall fence keeping us from fun, but they are more like an owner's manual giving us the information we need to function at a high level. There is nothing imposed or selfish or superficial about God's laws. They are the very fabric of the Universe. When God tells us what these laws are or points us in the right direction, wisdom obeys. Seeing the Creator's law as natural law opens the door to trust, which leads to obedience, which leads to healing.

God's Character

Who's got the whole world in His hands?

What kind of God is He?

It doesn't matter what name we give God, for He has thousands of names, but it does matter what we believe about Him. If we see God as a Dominance leader who wants control, who is willing to use force to get it, who cares about behavior more than character, who controls us through imposed laws and punishments, then we stress about rules and create theologies to hide us from God and force Him to let us into heaven. When we worship a controlling, severe, perfectionistic tyrant, tragically, we become just like the god we serve.

If we step into the light and choose to see God as Jesus demonstrated Him to be, an Influence leader who wants us to love Him and who is willing to give us the freedom to decide our own destiny, a God who cares more about our eternity than His own, the Creator who designed the Universe to run on natural laws, then we live in confidence, knowing that no matter what happens, all things work together for the good of those who trust in God.[17] We become accepting, joyful, and kind, just like the God we worship.

---

17   Romans 8:28

The Challenge

The old warrior stood before a vast multitude of people. They had followed him, bled with him, and conquered with him. Now it was his time to leave them. His heart ached as he saw their expectant faces. He had known their fathers, seen many of them grow up, and had led them all into the land of promise.

He scanned the surrounding fields and hills, verdant with crops and trees, and saw the majestic shrines and altars built to the local gods. He knew the enticing practices of the local religions with their beautiful dancing girls and mind numbing chants. He also knew the results of worshipping false gods—pain and death.

He looked up at the blue sky, and even though he couldn't see the God of Heaven, he believed God was watching. He knew God had fought their battles, conquered their enemies, and fulfilled every single one of His promises.

"The Lord will fight for you," Joshua's gravely voice whispered. "You need only to be still." His weathered face broke out into a broad smile as he remembered the many times that promise had brought him peace. It was true. God had always delivered him. *How can I help them understand?* Joshua thought. He took a deep breath and began, "My people, let me tell you a story."

The old warrior recounted the adventures of his life. He spoke of slavery and plagues, of crossing the Red Sea and dry deserts, of manna and miracles. Then Joshua told of walking through the Jordan River and around Jericho, of calling the sun to stand still and giant hailstones to fall like rain, of armies defeated and lands won. The people listened mesmerized. Many had witnessed these events, but to hear the old leader tell the stories was inspiring. Joshua had learned at the feet of Moses, had sat on Mt. Sinai, had spoken with the Angel of Heaven's armies. Now he was about to step down. Everyone present knew these were the old warrior's last official words. Soon he would join his fathers and rest in the dust.

Yet the grizzled veteran's voice was strong, and his eyes were sharp. His beard was white, but the muscles of his arms rippled as he gestured and spoke. Joshua's charisma glowed in the late afternoon light. Few men had his commanding presence. Joshua's quiet confidence belonged only to the men who spoke with God as a friend.

Joshua's mission was now complete. The nation had arrived and conquered the Promised Land. The people were no longer slaves, no longer wanderers. They were a mighty nation of conquerors, and it was all because of God's strong, right hand.

Joshua paused. Every eye locked on him. Every voice hushed to hear his words. Then with renewed passion the leader spoke, "Today choose the God you will serve. Will it be the pathetic false gods we have conquered into the dust, or will it be the Almighty God who gave us the victory? Will you bow to the gods of your enemies or to the God of your deliverance?"

His words echoed out over the people. They, too, saw the shrines and altars. They felt the invisible pull of lust and curiosity. They knew what they were supposed to do, but ...

Then Joshua spoke for the last time, "As for me and my house, we will serve the Lord."

The old leader stepped down and disappeared into the crowd. His words hung in the air, an invisible challenge, an impassioned call, an invitation for all to choose.[18]

Our Choice

Joshua's challenge echoes today. We must choose which God we will worship. Will it be the god of dominance whose laws are imposed and propped up with strict punishments? Or will we choose to worship a God of love, whose laws are built into the fabric of reality and who leads by example?

May we take our stand with the old warrior and declare, "As for me and my house, we will serve the Lord!"

---

18   Joshua 24

Main Points: I am fearless because ...

God is good.

God is an Influence Leader.

God's laws make sense and are in harmony with reality.

God's power protects and never controls.

God is with me.

Chapter 3

THE FREEDOM

"Then you will know the truth,
and the truth will set you free."[19]
—Jesus

The Prostitute

She saw the unusual men walking through the market. The men tried to look casual and blend in with the crowd, but their clothing and beards made them stand out. They were strong men whose muscles showed beneath their tunics, yet they looked incredibly nervous. She tilted her head, her beautiful brow furrowed. She tossed her long hair over her slim shoulder and studied the men more closely. Something didn't add up.

---

19   John 8:32 NIV

Most of the men came boldly to this quarter, knowing exactly what they wanted. They found the girl that pleased them, paid their money, and then disappeared into one of the brothel rooms. But these two men refused to make eye contact with any of the ladies. They looked completely out of place and had clearly taken a wrong turn.

Then out of the corner of her eye she saw the soldiers hustling from building to building obviously searching for someone.

She gasped and understood. Rumors whispered that Hebrew spies had entered the city. The King commanded everyone to be on the lookout and turn the foreigners in to the authorities. She looked back at the two men, who had also seen the soldiers. They were scanning the buildings, frantically searching for a hiding place. She knew what had to be done.

She swiftly stepped outside and took both men by the arms. "Gentlemen, let me get you out of this heat."

Her boldness surprised them, and they immediately followed her into her house. As soon as they were inside, she shut the door.

"Quickly!" she said. "Up the stairs!" She pushed the men up the narrow flight of stairs and out onto her roof. It was covered with stalks of flax drying in the sun. "Lie down and hide under these," she ordered.

One of the men grabbed her by the arm. "Why should we trust you?" he demanded.

"Because you have no choice!" she shot back. "Now hide." Just then fists pounded on her front door. The soldiers had arrived.

The two men scrambled under the flax. Quickly she spread the stalks over them, completely covering their bodies.

"Be quiet," she hissed then disappeared downstairs and opened the front door before the soldiers broke it down.

The two men prayed and listened as their hearts pounded in their chests. They heard muffled voices coming from downstairs, but no footsteps thumped up to the roof. After a long time, the sounds faded.

They heard soft footsteps and a quiet voice. "You're safe now," she said.

The spies rolled out from under the flax, stood, and brushed straw off their clothes. One of the men crept to the edge of the roof and peered cautiously down into the street.

The other man turned toward her. "Why did you do that?" he asked gently as he looked deeply into her shadowed eyes. Most men melted in the sultry heat of her beauty, but this man's gaze was strong and penetrating. He wasn't distracted by her jewelry or revealing dress. He was looking deeper.

The woman took a deep breath, calming her racing heart. "I have heard the stories of your people. Everyone is terrified of you." She paused and sat down. "Since I was a little girl I have loved the story of your God parting the Red Sea so you could walk across on dry ground. I have heard about the manna and the water from the rock, and how your God provides for you and protects you."

The man nodded and sat down beside her. His companion joined them and listened as the woman continued, "I also heard that many Egyptians left their gods and their homes to travel with you. Is that true? Do you accept outsiders in your camp?"

The men were silent for a few moments, and then one spoke. "Yes. We will take anyone who vows to worship the Lord our God and to obey His laws."

The woman pulled her knees to her chest and looked away. The men could sense an inner struggle, and one gently patted her shoulder. Slowly the woman turned and looked directly at him. Her eyes were fierce. "Anyone? Even someone like me?"

The man nodded with confidence. "Yes, anyone. Our God cares about a person's heart more than their past."

She swallowed hard. "I have been a prostitute in the temple of Ashtoreth since I was a young girl. I have done many things I am not proud of." She stopped. "But I know that your God is the true God, and I want to serve Him instead."

The man with gentle eyes reached out and took her hand in his. He looked deeply into her eyes. "I have done things I regret too, yet my God forgives me. He cleanses me. He loves me."

Tears sprang immediately to Rahab's eyes. "The moon goddess cares only about the money I earn her temple." She wiped her eyes and smiled. "I want to know your God."

The man smiled. "Can we stay here a few nights? We will sleep on the roof and pay for our lodging. When it is safe, we will leave."

She nodded. "Yes, I want to hear more."

The man introduced himself. "I'm Salmon."

"My name is Rahab."[20]

The Choice

In the entire city of Jericho, there was only one open heart, and it belonged to a prostitute. She was not a perfect person. She sold her body for a living, worshipped false gods, lied to the authorities, ate unclean foods, and did not keep the Sabbath, but something inside her soul recognized the light. She responded to it, and God accepted her with open arms. Now God would have welcomed every single person in Jericho, but only one was willing to let God change her heart.

Rahab accepted the new faith, changed her habits, and married a Hebrew. Her son grew up to be a godly man, proving that his mother abandoned her old life. In fact, Rahab's son, Boaz, rescued the loyal widow Ruth, and their grandson Jesse fathered David, the mighty king and ancestor of Jesus. God accepts everyone who accepts Him. The conquest of Cannan is a tragic story, not because God is a

---

20 Joshua 2

bloodthirsty tyrant bent on destruction, but because only one soul joined the winning team.

Every single person on planet earth must make a choice. The details vary, but the scenarios don't. We are dying, and God provides an escape, a life-saving remedy, an eternal solution. All must make a choice. Do we get on the ark or stay outside? Do we join the Hebrews or fight against them? Do we let Jesus into our hearts or lock the doors? Jesus explained this principle one day as He was teaching in the temple courts.

The Cornerstone

It had been a long day in the temple. As Jesus stood in front of the expectant crowd, He read each heart. Some wanted to hear His words and learn about God's kingdom. Others hoped to be healed. Some waited to trap Him so they could turn Him over to the Romans. He was about to begin another story when a group of religious teachers pushed their way to the front. The people jumped back and bowed their heads in respect. The teachers of the law wore expensive clothes and carried themselves with dignity, but their eyes dripped with poison. They silently stood with their arms crossed. Their disapproving presence transformed the scene. Little children ran back to their mothers, and people who wished to be healed shrank back into the crowd. No one asked any more questions.

Jesus looked at these men who were supposed to draw people closer to God. Now they were doing their best to push people away. He leaned against a massive cornerstone. Jesus patted it.

Everyone knew the story of the original cornerstone in Solomon's temple. That stone was four times larger than this one. Some said that it was so polished a person could see their reflection. During the construction, the giant stone had been delivered but not labeled. Its massive bulk kept getting in the way of the workers. They had no idea what to do with it. They tried to fit it in the walls several times, but the monstrosity stuck out awkwardly. Finally, the foreman ordered it to be shoved aside. It was so large that no one wanted to transport it back to the quarry, so someone covered it in supplies. Soon the stone was forgotten.

At last, the day came to lay the cornerstone. This stone was the most important piece of the walls because it would hold the most weight. It must be perfect with no cracks or weaknesses; otherwise, the colossal stress would crush it. If it failed, then other stones in the temple would crash down, and the building would be ruined.

The workers scrambled to find the cornerstone. Many blocks were tried and even put into place, but none passed the test. Some were too small, while others were scratched or cracked under pressure. Finally, someone remembered the abandoned block, and the builders hauled the giant piece into place.

The once-rejected stone fit beautifully. The immense weight of the building was perfectly balanced and supported. When people heard the story of the stone, it became famous. Teachers of the law used the stone as a symbol for the coming Messiah. For generations, worshipers reverently touched it and prayed for the coming Redeemer.

Now Jesus placed His hand on the cornerstone of Herod's temple and said, "The stone the builders rejected has become the cornerstone." He paused, looked directly at the teachers, and leaned forward, "Whoever falls onto this stone will be broken. Whoever this stone falls on will be crushed."

The crowd murmured. The teachers glared. And Jesus sighed, looked at the cornerstone one more time, and walked out of the temple.[21]

The Warning

Jesus talked to the teachers in symbols and code. He knew they understood Him perfectly. The religious leaders knew the cornerstone represented the Messiah, but they didn't know that to follow the Messiah, a person must be broken and humbled. They longed for a proud Messiah who would fulfill their desires for power, control, and wealth, but in order to gain the blessings, the teachers of the law wrongly believed that they had to earn it.

---

21   Matthew 21:42-44, Psalm 118:22

One reason why the religious leaders and teachers burdened the nation with so many man-made rules was to herd the people into behavior that would keep God happy. They viewed the sin of idol worship as the cause of the destruction of Solomon's temple and their nation's captivity, but instead of seeing their separation from God as the cause of their nation's tragedy, they blamed God for punishing them. When the Israelites persisted in idol worship, they were in effect, rejecting God, so He accepted their choice and pulled His protective presence away. As always, evil rushed in to fill the void and wreaked havoc on Israel. The root of their pain was their choice to separate themselves from God.

Jesus saw the leaders' ignorance and attempted to enlighten them by pointing them to the cornerstone. In a flash, the religious teachers understood the meaning. Jesus was inviting them to humble themselves, to be broken. Jesus was chipping away at their fear-based religion propped up to appease a wrathful god and showing them that God would support. But they were too proud, too tied to their ideas, and the teachers refused to turn back. Yet they understood the warning. If they rejected Jesus as the supporting Cornerstone, then they would be crushed by their decision.

The religious leaders looked directly into Jesus' eyes and saw the truth. They knew He was the Messiah, but He wasn't the kind of god they wanted. They turned their backs on His light and embraced the fatal darkness. They chose to reject God as revealed in Jesus, to fight against Him, and finally to crucify Him.

They succeeded, but in their victory, they tasted no joy. In their triumph, they felt no thrill. They felt nothing, only the weight of their choice as it slowly crushed their souls.

The Pattern

The Bible is full of a repeating pattern. God presents the truth in love and gives people the freedom to choose. God gives clear instructions on how to live the best life. God sees a coming disaster and always provides a way of escape. God warns. God pleads. He does everything possible to convince people to change their destructive course of action, but because God values freedom, He always lets humans make their own decisions. God is a God of love. Love and freedom always co-exist. When freedom is taken away, true love evaporates.

But many people reject God's wisdom and suffer the natural consequences of their harmful choices.

Many critics point to the invasion of Canaan and claim that God is a monster who ordered genocide. But under investigation, we discover the same choice/consequence pattern used before the flood. During the time of Abraham, the inhabitants of Canaan had a strong view of right and wrong.[22]

---

22   Genesis 20:1-18

In Genesis 15:16, God says that their sins had not reached maturity. This means that the culture was moving away from God but had not completely severed their connection to Him. They needed time to make their final decision, so God sent Abraham's family to Egypt and gave the Canaanites four hundred years of grace.

During that four hundred year time frame, the Canaanites grew more evil. Their religious rites included human and child sacrifices, sexual abuse, and dark spiritualism. God gave strong warnings to wake the Canaanites up by displaying His power in the ten plagues where He systematically destroyed the mightiest gods of the Egyptians.

Egypt was a world power whose wealth and influence impacted all other nations. When the Israelites were miraculously delivered by the God of the Hebrews from the strongest nation on earth, everyone knew about it. The Cannannites heard about the path through the sea, the fire on the mountain, the manna in the morning, the water from the rock, and they were amazed. No one could deny the truth, the overwhelming evidence. The God of the Hebrews was real, and He was powerful.

When Joshua and the Israelites crossed through the Jordan River on dry ground during the rainy season, it was like the animals marching aboard the ark, unmistakable proof that a God existed who fought for His people. Instead of protecting and providing for the people, the selfish gods of Cannan demanded endless sacrifice. These gods used their people. They did not deliver their people. The contrast could not have been more clear. When the Israelites crossed the Jordan River, every inhabitant in Cannan had the same opportunity. The tragedy is that only Rahab made the correct choice. Every other nation chose to reject the true God and attack His people.[23] Their decision to attack the Cornerstone resulted in their destruction, while Rahab's decision to accept the gift placed her in the lineage of the Messiah.

God's Power

God is powerful, but He is a God of love. God never uses His power selfishly. Jesus walked on water, healed the sick, fed thousands, and brought the dead to life. Jesus didn't use His power to turn stones to bread in the desert. He didn't use power to defeat the Roman invaders. He didn't use power when He was arrested, beaten, whipped, or nailed to the cross. Jesus reached the limits of human endurance, and He could have used His godlike power to stop His enemies, but He didn't. Instead, Jesus proved that God can be trusted with ultimate power.

Many times in the Old Testament we see God's power defending His people from evil. David and

---

23   The Gibeonites, through trickery and lies, did make an alliance with Israel. They were the only people group who did not try to destroy God's people. See Joshua 9.

Goliath, the Fiery Furnace, and the Red Sea are prime examples. Other times we see His power used to teach and protect a nation from corruption. Uzzah touching the ark of the covenant, Dathan and Abiram's rebellion, and Elijah's three year drought all show God using His power to put His people back on track. In any story where God looks controlling or selfish or tyrannical, we must dig deeper. The prophet Malchai said that the Lord does not change.[24] The God of the Old Testament is the same God who preached the Sermon on the Mount. We must see every Bible story through the lens of Jesus' life and teaching. As we hear the sermons, witness the miracles, and listen at the feet of Jesus, we can see God clearly. Then at the foot of the cross, we can finally understand the ultimate truth of the universe. God is good. God is selfless. God is love.

TWO STORIES FROM THE WILD WEST

The Hold Up

The stagecoach rocked back and forth as the wheels rolled and bumped over the desert tracks. The passengers were hot, and the horses were tired. Everet took out his dirty handkerchief and wiped his brow. Then he looked out the window at the towering mesas and shimmering sands. He thought about his

---

24   Malachi 3:6

dreams of coming to the west and helping people. Everet was a recent graduate from medical school and wanted to do his part to bring health and healing to the wild west. He smiled as he daydreamed about being called Doc and saving lives.

A loud crack jolted him back to reality. The stage lurched to a stop, and the horses whinnied. Everet stuck his head out the window and what he saw made his heart stop cold.

Four men on horseback with bandanas covering their faces and pistols in their hands blocked the way. Everet jerked his head back into the stagecoach. His face was as white as his wet shirt, and his hands shook.

Just then, someone ripped open the door, and a man in a dark hat with fierce eyes leaned in. The bandit pointed his Colt Peacemaker right at Everet and said, "This is a hold up."

As Everet stepped out of the stage, he frantically searched for an escape. Two robbers rifled through the passengers' trunks looking for valuables while another questioned the stage driver about the cash box under his seat. The fourth man waved his pistol at the passengers.

"Empty your pockets and toss any money or jewelry you have on the ground," the bandit barked.

The passengers quickly obeyed. Everet pulled out a delicate gold locket. He opened it and looked at the small picture inside. It was a portrait of his twin sister, Evie, who had died while he was away at school. Before Everet left, his mother had given him Evie's locket.

"It was her most prized possession," his mother had said with tears in her eyes. "Evie would have wanted you to have it." Everet couldn't bear to part with it.

The robber noticed the locket. "Give it here, boy," he growled and held out a dirty hand.

Everet looked up and pleaded, "Sir, this was my sister's and is very dear to me. She passed away."

The robber snatched the watch from Everet's hand and cackled, "It's very dear to me too. This piece of work will buy me a lot of drinks." The bandit clipped the locket open and whistled. "Hello beautiful." The thief leered at the photograph and licked his lips. Then he slipped the locket into his vest pocket and turned his attention to another passenger.

Everet blinked back tears and clenched his fists. Then he snapped.

He rushed the man with the gun and grabbed it. The gun exploded, and both men tumbled to the ground. They rolled in the dirt and struggled to pin each other down. Everet felt someone grab his shoulders with a vice grip and pick him up. He felt weightless for a moment as he flew through the air and then crashed onto a rock. A flash of pain and light blurred his vision, and then everything went black.

The Choice

When Everet woke up, it was dark and his hands were tied behind his back. He moaned. His head throbbed, and he could taste blood in his mouth.

"Well, look who decided to wake up," a scornful voice shot out of the darkness. Everet heard heavy footsteps and the clink of spurs. A pair of boots stopped in front of his face. Everet rolled over and struggled to sit up.

There was the scratch of a match and a flame lit up the face of a man holding a cigarette. Everet saw a long black mustache and dark eyes that held death. Everet swallowed hard.

The man rose up and took a long draft on his cigarette. He slowly blew the smoke out and said, "What you did today was dumb, boy. Charlie could have killed you easy." The man paused and puffed on his cigarette. "But it showed me that you got guts, and that's something I like."

The robber pulled out his revolver, and Everet heard the metallic click as the bandit cocked the gun. "So I'm gonna give you a choice." He leveled the gun at Everet. "You can join my gang or you can meet your Maker."

Everet looked at the gun and made his decision.

The Scout

There was no denying it. Tom was lost. He pulled back the reins on his horse and looked around again. Everything looked the same. All he could see was short stubby cactus patches and red rocks. He tried to lick his parched lips, but his tongue was as dry as sand. Tom squinted up at the sky. Buzzards circled overhead in the cloudless sky.

Tom slid off his horse and took the reins. He trudged ahead, his boots scraping against the rocks and his head hung in despair.

Just then his horse, Comanche, stopped and whinnied. Something was wrong. Tom looked up in fear, and his blood ran cold.

Dark smoke rose from the remains of a ranch. Tom stumbled forward, and the sight that met his eyes broke his heart. The barn was burned. The animals were gone. And someone needed to bury the bodies.

Tom saw a shovel laying on the ground near a water trough. He picked it up and got to work.

Later that evening, he scrounged some food and drank some water from the well. He couldn't stay here for the night. The bandits may return, and he knew how cruel they could be.

Tom swung up onto Commanche and trotted into the twilight. The moon began to rise behind him, and the desert turned cold.

"Hold it, pilgrim," a sharp voice cut through the still air. A man on a horse emerged from behind a large rock. The moon caught the glint of a raised pistol.

Tom gulped and put his hands up in the air. "I ain't got no money. Honest, mister." Tom's breathing was fast. He knew he couldn't escape. The man had a gun, and the moon was bright.

"Well," the man holstered his gun. "I reckon you ain't one of them bandits or else you wouldn't startle so easily."

The stranger made a soft clicking sound, and his horse moved closer to Tom. The cowboy pushed his hat back off his forehead and spit into the darkness.

"Put your hands down. I ain't a bandit. I saw the smoke, but you got to it before I did. I was going to ride down and help you but stumbled on the bandit's camp." The stranger leaned forward in his saddle, and the leather creaked. "They was watching you."

Chills ran down Tom's spine, and he nervously bit his lip. A horse cried out in the distance, and the sound of hoofs striking rocks drifted on the cool night breeze.

Tom tried to sound brave, but his voice shook. "That's them, ain't it?"

"Most likely," the big man said. "I slipped past them, come late afternoon. I don't know why, but I came to help you." The man stuck out his hand. "The name's Jake."

Tom weakly shook Jake's hand and introduced himself.

"Mighty nice to meet you," Jake said. Then something caught his attention, and he peered into the darkness. "You can ride with me," Jake whispered and started to move off. Tom looked back toward the ranch and then up at the hills where he had heard the bandits' horses. Then he looked at Jake. The cowboy had stopped and was waiting.

"They're getting closer." Jake pointed his gun in the direction of the hills. In the moonlight on his horse, Jake seemed larger than life. Tom was lost. He had no gun and no chance by himself, yet he was frozen in fear.

Jake trotted his horse back to Tom. "I ain't gonna force you to do anything, but you're about out of time, pilgrim."

Suddenly there was a loud crack and a bullet whistled past Tom's shoulder, followed by a wild cackle.

"I almost got 'em!" a voice shrieked.

Jake's pistol was in his hand. He fired two shots in the night and whirled his horse around.

"You coming?" he shouted.

Tom looked at the gun and made his decision.

Who Is Holding the Gun?

In both stories, a man holding a gun gave an invitation. The robber invited Everet into his gang, and Jake offered to help Tom escape the bandits. Both

Jake and the robber held a gun, but the character of the two men was very different. In one hand, the gun was a threat; in another hand, the gun was a promise of safety.

Many times salvation is presented by well meaning preachers in a similar way to the first story. God offers us a chance to join Him, but there is a threat. If we refuse God's gift of mercy, then He will be forced to punish us because He is just. Romans 6:23 states that the wages of sin is death, and this argument places the responsibility for that death in God's hands. He is the Judge, and He decides our punishment. If we don't join God, then He will condemn us, and we will go to hell. In this traditional view of the salvation story, God is holding the gun, and it's pointed at us. This god is not safe. This god is not love.

The true story of salvation is very different. Like Tom, we are lost and in danger. God rides in with His glorious power and offers us a way out, a rescue. Remember in the story at the Red Sea, God provided an escape through the water. If the Hebrews stayed on the beach, they would have been killed by the Egyptians, *not God*. We don't have to join God, but if we refuse, we will die. In the true version of salvation, it is not God who will kill us, but our sins. Sin brings death.[25] God can save us from that death, but we must choose to ride with Him. This God is safe. This God is love.

---

25   James 1:15

The Boat

What more could I do? the old man thought as he looked over the crowd. Their upturned faces betrayed their emotions—disgust, amusement, hatred. Not one friendly face stood out. He lifted his gaze toward heaven. *Lord, please open their eyes,* he prayed.

Just then a woman screamed, pointing toward the forest. Everyone's attention swung down the valley. Two giant elephants strode out of the shadows and trumpeted. The powerful beasts walked side by side as if led by an invisible hand. People scrambled to get out of the way. The elephants shook their heads and waved their trunks at the panicked crowd, but they did not charge. Instead they walked straight up the ramp and into the giant boat. Noah hurried after them and looked inside just in time to see the pair calmly walk into a large stall. His son, Shem, shut the door to the stall. He smiled at his father.

"You were right," Shem said nonchalantly. "God will provide."

Noah's family had been discussing for weeks how they could capture the animals and get them onto the ark. Japheth was in favor of traps and lures, while Ham had argued for hiring professional hunters to do the job. Noah had prayed and prayed, but he had received no real answers, only a calm reassurance that God would provide. Faithfully, Noah told his family to trust in God's help. God had handled every imaginable problem during the 120 year building project. Each time they ran into a wall of impossibility, God had taken care of them. Noah knew that it would be no different with the animals.

Noah smiled and said, "Go get your brothers, Shem. I have a feeling this is just the beginning." He turned to walk back outside and almost ran into a pair of tigers who growled at him but did not pounce. The tigers padded to a stall and waited for Shem to shut them inside.

Noah shook his head. "Lord, You are so amazing!" He walked outside more carefully this time, and what he saw took his breath away. For miles and miles a solid line of animals snaked across the valley stretching up into the foothills. Most of the animals walked side by side, but some animals came in small groups. Noah watched rabbits, bears, kangaroos, and crocodiles march calmly past him into the shelter of the ark. Predators showed no aggression, and their prey showed no fear. Occasionally, an animal would roar or bellow or squeak, but for the most part all the animals quietly and peacefully crawled, plodded, and hopped into the ark.

Noah looked back at the crowd. Their faces were pale in disbelief. Soon people were running madly from the nearby town to see this miraculous spectacle. The crowd quickly doubled in size. Noah's heart raced with hope, *Maybe now they will listen to me*, he thought.

Then he noticed an ominous cloud darkening the sky. He felt a surge of fear. *Oh no! The flood has begun!*

Noah squinted toward the cloud, wondering at its irregular pattern. The dark shape tumbled and shifted, rising up and then diving down. It was too fast and too sporadic to be a cloud. Then he heard it. Bird calls, hundred and thousands of different songs echoing in the skies above. The cloud was a flock of birds, a cacophony of shrieks and tweets.

A thousand wings beat the air as the massive flock flew up the valley and began to circle the ark. Pairs of birds split off and flew into the large upper deck window. Noah ducked inside and saw his daughter-in-law rushing up the ladder. Shem must have told her what to do.

He stepped back out and stood in reverent awe. Never before in earth's brief history had so many living creatures come to one place.

Noah took a deep breath. He could see God's plan. The animals and birds had brought the largest crowd that had ever come to the ark. This would be the final invitation, the last chance to get on the ark.

"Lord, please fill me with Your words and Your spirit," Noah breathed. Even though he was surrounded by a spectacle that would never be seen again in world history, the old man bowed his head and prayed.

Noah prayed as he had never prayed before. He knew what was coming. The visions of the flood still gave him nightmares. For one hundred and twenty years he had tried so hard to make the people believe him, but so far his only converts were his own family. All of his neighbors, old coworkers, and even his dear friends called him crazy. But now surely things would be different. The animals would open their eyes to the truth. The truth that God loved them and wanted to save them.

Noah looked up. The huge flock of birds had finally funneled into the ark's window. Two dogs trotted up the ramp wagging their tails. They were the very last animals. The dogs paused at the entrance to the ark, and one licked Noah's hand as if to say thank you. Then they bounded inside.

Now it was the people's turn.

Noah stood alone at the giant door of the ark. "Fill me, Lord," he whispered, and then Noah began to speak. His words were different this time. He had always preached with passion, but today he was absolutely electric. Noah felt the power surge through his body. God was with him.

Noah spoke first about the pain in the world, of the massacres, the plagues, the wars, and the diseases. He spoke about the Garden and the Angel of Light that stood at its entrance. He spoke of the coming flood and God's passionate plea for all to come into the ark of safety.

The crowd was riveted. There was no jeering this time. No one threw food or shouted lewd comments about Noah's wife. There was just silence. Noah gave his audience everything he had because he knew this was their last opportunity. Noah called out to friends in the crowd, people he loved, neighbors who had eaten at his table, friends he had known for hundreds of years. Noah talked about God's character of forgiveness and how grace is free. He invited everyone to come into the ark.

He pointed to a famous hunter. "Abner," he said, "You taught me that animals can sense a change in the weather before we do. You told me to always be aware of their behavior, for one day it would save my life." Noah paused. "Today is that day, my friend."

Noah could see a battle raging in Abner's face. The great hunter was a man of mighty strength, and if he joined Noah, then surely more would follow. But then something changed in Abner's eyes as the struggle ended. The internal battle within his heart was over. Abner glared at Noah and then spit.

Noah's heart sank, but he refused to give up. He turned to another friend, and another, and another. But each answer was the same. For each individual, there was a brief internal conflict but then complete rejection. Noah's shoulders slumped. If humans still refused to trust and obey even after the miracle of the animals, what more could God possibly do?

Noah tried one final time.

"God is good. He loves each and every one of you. That is why He has provided this way of escape from the coming destruction. The door is open. The entrance is free. Come, my friends. Enter into this ark and find peace and safety. Come and join me!" Noah held out his hand to the crowd but was met with stony silence. He could feel the very presence of God. It seemed to radiate around the ark, but he realized he was the only one who felt it. No one else's heart was open.

Then Noah heard sinister laughter. It started near the back of the throng but soon spread. Noah could sense the menacing darkness rise as the mob pointed at the old prophet and mocked him. Some yelled foul threats and curses while others threw rocks. Then a group of men with clubs in their hands pushed their way to the front and stomped up the plank. Their intention was clear. They were out for blood.

"Noah!" God's voice spoke. "Get inside the ark." Noah obeyed. As he stepped inside, a few rocks narrowly missed his head and smashed hard against the wood. Noah's family watched him anxiously, huddled together in fear. They could all hear the footsteps of the men coming up the ramp.

"How do we shut the door?" Ham asked in a panicked voice. "It's too heavy for us to shut from the inside!" The men's footsteps were closer, and Shem reached over and picked up a rake.

"We may have to fight, Father," he said grimly.

"God will provide," Noah said calmly. "He is our Defender."

Just then a bolt of lightning struck the entrance. There was a terrific crash of thunder, and Noah fell backwards. His ears rang, and his vision blurred. It seemed that the sun itself had crashed in front of the ark. Noah shielded his eyes and squinted into the brilliant light.

Standing in the entrance was a mighty angel of light who throbbed with power and energy. The angel held a huge sword of fire and stood ready to fight. Noah heard the tumble of footsteps as the thugs rushed back down the ramp in panic. The angel lowered the sword, nodded to Noah, and then stepped outside.

A loud rumble shook the floor of the ark as the giant door began to move. The massive door creaked and groaned as it swung shut, vibrations echoing through the rafters. Its heavy slam sent a rush of air against Noah's face. He bowed his head.

Noah reached for his wife's hand and held it tightly. "And so it begins," Noah murmured as he looked at his wife. She nodded and wrapped her arm around his waist.

All the years of planning and building were over. The flood would come soon. Noah knelt down on the wooden floor, and his family followed his example. Everyone was looking at him. Noah's heart pounded in his chest as he closed his eyes and said a prayer of thanksgiving. When he had finished, his family stayed on their knees, warm peace flooding each of their hearts.

"The storm is coming," Noah said. Then he smiled as he stood up. "But God is with us, and we have nothing to fear."[26]

Our Chance

There is another flood coming. Soon the world will be engulfed with chaos. The only safe place will be in the ark. This time there is no wooden boat to enter, but we have what the ark symbolized: a relationship with Jesus. Our relationship starts like Rahab's, with a desire for more light, for more hope, for more love. Our rough edges are broken away by the Cornerstone as we mature and experience God's peace. We finally bear fruit, and our characters will begin to reflect His nature. When the storm hits and life gets rough, like Noah, we will say, "God will provide," and peace will fill our souls.

If you want this peace, if you want to leave a god of threats and violence to follow a God of love and freedom, if you want to begin that relationship, then it starts with a simple prayer:

Jesus, I love You, and I trust in You. I believe that God is good, and that He will provide. I want to follow You. Amen.

If you prayed that prayer, hang on tight. The adventure is about to begin.

---

26   Genesis 6, 7

Main Points: I am fearless because ...
God is good.
God gives everyone the freedom to choose.
God will save everyone who accepts His
healing from sin.
God is with me.

Chapter 4

THE DESIRE

"I want you to show love, not offer
sacrifices. I want you to know Me
more than I want burnt offerings."[27]
—God

The Visit

The Queen paced back and forth. She was nervous.
She took a deep breath and forced herself to be still.
She sat down next to a fountain and looked around.

The courtyard was painted blue, and live flowers
climbed the pillars. A colorful peacock called and
strode out from behind one of the pillars. He fanned
out his wide tail, showing off for the Queen as his
feet clicked across the polished marble floor. She
smiled and trailed her fingers through the water of

---

27   Hosea 6:6 NLT

the fountain. She gasped in delight as she noticed shimmering diamonds at the bottom of the pool. The diamonds were set in the shape of constellations and sparkled in the morning light. Beautiful music drifted in from somewhere over the walls, and she heard music and laughter.

This palace was far different from hers back home. She was rich, and her courtyards were impressive, but they paled in comparison to this extravagance. Then she heard light footsteps approaching, so she arose and watched a regal young woman wearing a flowing purple robe with golden embroidery glide into the courtyard.

She must be someone important, the Queen thought as her practiced eye took in the jeweled bracelets on the woman's wrists and the slender crown of gold that sat lightly on a smooth forehead.

The woman bowed elegantly. "I am Tirssa, the King's official receptionist. I will take you to him now."

The Queen nodded her head, surprised that this woman was a servant and not royalty, then followed Tirssa down a corridor lined with golden shields, through a manicured garden filled with fruit trees and a bubbling stream, and into a room that shone like the noonday sun. The Queen's mouth dropped open, and for one moment she forgot herself as she gazed at the sheer wealth on display.

Gold gilded the walls, and a chandelier with dozens of lamps filled the room with dancing light.

Exotic animal skins rested on delicate pieces of furniture, while the rich carpet on the floor swallowed her feet. She looked up. A splendid pastoral scene of a couple walking with a god stretched across the ceiling. Everything shimmered with jewels. She was so enamored, the Queen failed to see the man sitting in a chair watching her.

"I will leave you here, your Highness," Tirssa said with a bow.

"Thank you," the Queen stammered. *The cost of a room like this could outfit an entire navy*, she thought. Then she saw him.

His eyes shone with intelligence, and she could feel the charisma that so many had talked about. The Queen bowed in respect, for the king's reputation was legendary. He was the famous architect and the genius inventor. He was the poet of the East and the wisest man in all the earth.

The King stood smiling and walked to her. "Welcome," he said as he honored her with a deep bow. "I am Solomon."

The Temple

The next few days whirled by for the Queen of Sheba. Solomon was the perfect gentleman and gave her a tour of Jerusalem. He showed her the city's ingenious water system, markets teeming with goods from far away lands, and his enormous complex of stables filled with magnificent horses. As she rode through the streets next to him in an inlaid ivory chariot, she marveled at the health, happiness, and prosperity of the citizens of Jerusalem.

The Queen was full of questions, but first she tested him with difficult riddles. Solomon laughed and answered them with ease though he never gave her the expected solution. The King always came up with a unique answer, one that made complete sense. Then the Queen grilled Solomon about diplomacy, politics, and economics trying to unveil the secret to his colossal success. He held nothing back and patiently explained the principles he used everyday. Her mind soaked up everything Solomon shared. Slowly the Queen stopped testing him and began to ask questions from the deepest part of her soul. Solomon became her teacher, and she was the eager pupil.

One day standing on a balcony, she looked out over the city and saw the temple. It was glorious. The white marble shone in the bright sunlight. The Queen was not allowed to go inside its sacred precincts, but she had a wonderful view from his palace.

"Tell me about your religion," she cocked her head to one side. "Tell me about your temple."

Solomon's face changed. The lighthearted humor melted into a respectful nobility. He walked over to her and leaned on the balcony railing then pointed to the temple.

"That's not my temple," he said humbly. "I wish they wouldn't call it Solomon's Temple." He was silent for a moment, lost in thought. Then he glanced at her and began the most important conversation of the Queen's life.

"That temple is a symbol. It is a shadow of the truth." Just then the evening trumpet blew. The majestic notes soared over the city, calling everyone to stop their business and pray. Solomon bowed his head reverently, and his lips moved silently.

When he had finished his prayer, he looked at the Queen. She could feel his genuine care for her. "Tell me about your gods," he said. "Do they require sacrifices?"

The Queen nodded. As the monarch of her land, she was also the high priestess. She told Solomon about her desert gods and spoke of their greatness and wrath. As high priestess, the Queen was responsible for the most important sacrifices to the gods. If she failed to perform the sacred rites perfectly, then the gods would rip away their blessings and deliver her kingdom to the desert, to be swallowed by snakes and sand. The Queen had never told anyone her true feelings about her religion, but with Solomon she felt safe. She sadly confessed that her life was filled with fear and dread. She was terrified that if she was not good enough, then the gods would punish not only her, but also the innocent people in her kingdom. She tried hard to be good enough, but it exhausted her and filled her with dark foreboding. She felt no peace, only the nagging pull of a perfection always out of her reach.

Solomon listened attentively. When she had finished, the King placed a comforting hand on her shoulder. "You are a good queen," he said warmly. "You long for peace and prosperity for your people. You don't have to live in fear. May I tell you about my God?"

The Queen nodded and somehow felt lighter after sharing her heart with Solomon. He sat on an elegant bench, and motioned for her to join him.

"A long time ago, in a land far away … " Solomon told her a story about a garden with a tree and a snake.

The Queen interrupted him. "Is this story pictured on the ceiling in the gold room?"

He smiled and nodded. "I had it painted there to remind me of the lesson Adam and Eve learned." Solomon went on to tell the story. She was fascinated. When he finished, the King asked a question, "What is the moral of the story?"

It was obvious to the Queen, "Disobey God, and He will punish you."

Solomon shook his head, "Go deeper into the story. Before they ate the fruit, what happened in their hearts?"

She paused to think. "They listened to the snake?" she asked.

"Before they stood under the tree," Solomon leaned forward, "What happened in their hearts?"

Then in one moment of clarity, the Queen understood. "They doubted God's goodness. To go to the tree, to listen to the snake, Adam and Eve first had to doubt." She slowly nodded.

"They took their eyes off God's goodness, then they were susceptible to the lie." Solomon said softly. "That's why they ran away when God came to the garden that evening. They were afraid of Him." Then the King rose and looked toward the temple. "God had to take away the fear, so He gave us the gift of the sacrifice."

The Queen wrinkled her nose, "That doesn't make sense. The sacrifice is our gift to the gods. We give our best to earn their blessings."

Solomon smiled. "That's how it works in other religions, but ours is different. The sacrifice is a symbol, not a payment. God promised Adam and Eve that He would come and die in their place. They needed to understand that sin separates us from God, the source of life. Because of that separation from God, we die. They needed to be afraid of sin, not God."

The Queen listened intently, and Solomon continued. "When we commit wrong, whether it is in our hearts or our actions, we must take a perfect lamb to the altar. We are to place our hands on it, confess our sins, and kill it ourselves."

Solomon winced. "That perfect, innocent lamb is a symbol of God's Messiah. My sins will kill my Savior." He sighed, "To sacrifice breaks my heart. It makes me hate my sin. It humbles me, yet gives me hope. The sacrifice reminds me of God's promise, of His love, and that takes away my fear."

The King pointed to the temple and spoke of the giant cornerstone, the bronze wash basin, the colors of the curtains, the golden furniture, and the ark of the covenant. Each one highlighted a different aspect of God's character. Solomon's face lit up as he explained. The Queen had heard Solomon talk about his wealth, his palace, and his accomplishments. But now he glowed with joy and energy, as if his God was living in his heart.

Then Solomon told her about the day he had dedicated the temple. She let herself be carried away with his innocent enthusiasm. The King talked about the people, the music, the sacrifices. Then he spoke of the Presence.

Solomon's eyes flashed as he told her how the glory of God permeated the new temple. He described the bright light of God's holy presence, pulsing with energy, washing over the people with waves of brilliance, and turning the building so white it glowed like the sun.

Lost in the rapture of the moment, Solomon whispered. "Immanuel, God with us. We don't need to fear Him. We just need to love Him. That is what this temple is all about. It is the most beautiful building in the world for one reason, it will draw people here, just like you. Then we can share the good news about our God and His loving principles that can bring peace to our souls and to the world. We can point to the lamb on the altar and share the promise of the Messiah."

Solomon turned to the Queen. "The Messiah will be perfect, so we don't have to be. The Messiah will trust God completely and show us how to truly live. Our religion is not about work. It's about worship. The more I focus on God and His true character, the more I become like Him."

"Is that the secret to your success and wisdom?" she asked as she walked back to the railing and stared at the temple. "Does all this come from your God?"

Solomon nodded. "Yes. It's not about me. My wisdom, my position, my wealth are all gifts from God, and I must use them to help others." Then Solomon became serious, "But if I ever turn my gifts to selfish purposes, I will destroy myself and my people. That is why worship is so important. When I truly worship, I lose myself in God."

The Queen's soul ached for the experience Solomon spoke about. Her religion was either formal and dry or chaotic and out of control. It was never vibrant. It never fed her soul. She wanted to know Solomon's God. "How do I worship your God?" she asked hesitantly.

Solomon smiled. "Trust in the Lord with all your heart and do not depend on your own understanding. Seek His will in all you do, and He will show you which path to take."[28]

---

28   Proverbs 3:5, 6

They were silent for a long time, lost in their own thoughts. Then the Queen spoke, "I want to trust in the God you know. I want to believe and feel what I see in you. What must I do?"

"True worship comes from trusting hearts." Solomon placed a hand on his chest. "Genuine worship comes from here. It's not about rituals or rules. It's about love."

When the Queen of Sheba left Jerusalem, she was content. She left with far more wealth than when she had arrived and had learned so much in a few short days with King Solomon. The Queen felt peaceful and happy. She patted the satchel of sacred scrolls that Solomon had given her. "They're full of amazing stories," he grinned. "Read them and learn to trust God even more."

As her camel came to the top of a hill, she turned and looked back. The temple gleamed in the early morning light, and she faintly heard the trumpet's call to worship. She looked up at the pink and blue sky and smiled.

"I trust in You, God," she said. "I trust in You."[29]

The Gift

As we watch the Queen of Sheba disappear into the shadows of time, we know that she was saved. She never sacrificed at the temple. She didn't eat

---

29   1 Kings 10:1-13, 2 Chronicles 9:1-12

a kosher diet. She didn't become a Jew, but she did believe. She trusted in God, and her fear faded.

The Queen saw that true religion is not about rules, rituals, and performances. True religion is about the heart, the character, and genuine worship. She saw the stark contrast between her old gods and her new God. One god demanded sacrifice, while the other God *was* the sacrifice. One god ruled through fear, while the other led with love. One god promised salvation only for those who worked hard and became good enough, while the other God promised salvation for everyone who believed. One god demanded gifts, while the other God *was* the gift.

One of the leftover beliefs from the old, pagan religions is that salvation is mainly a deliverance from torture and death. King Solomon, however, had it right when he told the Queen of Sheba about *Immanuel*, God with Us. He shifted her focus from what she was being saved *from* to *Whom* she was being saved by. Instead of fixating on hellfire, he pointed her to the Helper. This shift ennobles the worshipper. True salvation restores intimacy with God. It's letting Jesus into our heart.

Everything at the temple pointed to the Messiah, who would set the Universe straight about God's character. God used each symbol to remind humanity of our original purpose—to enjoy an intimate, trusting relationship with God. Salvation closes the gap between heaven and our hearts. It heals our minds so that we no longer serve God out of fear or reject Him out of ignorance. Instead we run to Him with open arms.

The Conquest

God's original plan for the nation of Israel was to use them to conquer the world, but this conquest would be like no other. God would bless His people with vitality, wealth, and wisdom. People outside the Jewish nation would see their monumental achievements and come to learn. Solomon's wisdom and faithfulness to God brought prosperity and blessings. When seekers like the Queen of Sheba traveled to Jerusalem in search of the secrets to his success, Solomon had the perfect opportunity to share the good news about God's character, to explain the symbols of his religion, to share stories of God's deliverance of all who trust Him. God's plan was for all people to come and learn. Then they could freely choose to accept or reject the new light. God would use no force, no manipulation, no deception. This is how God planned to conquer the world and push back the forces of evil.

The Bible has many stories of outsiders who were welcomed into the Hebrew culture because they chose to worship the Living God: Rahab the prostitute, Ruth the Moabite, Uriah the Hittite, and even Ziporah, Moses' wife. God conquered all these people with love. They came voluntarily. They saw the truth, and they surrendered. God's way was so full of light and warmth, it drew them to the truth. They were set free from religions of work and stepped into the glow of worship.

What Does God Want?

God wants intimacy with each of us. We were built for it. Babies who are held and cuddled thrive. Lovers who gaze into each other's eyes deepen their bond. Old friends who simply sit together strengthen their friendship. Humans thrive emotionally, mentally, and physically when our need for intimate connection is met. God created us for connection, and He wants to share life with us. But most of us don't want what God wants. We feel a hole in our soul and know that something is missing, but we mistakenly search for fulfillment by walking away from God. We think contentment comes from money, power, sex, applause, accomplishment, or some other mirage. We try to earn our keep and prove to the world that we are worthwhile. No matter how much we achieve, we feel broken, exhausted, and empty.

God calls to us in our desperation. "Come to Me all you who are tired and lonely, who are lost and afraid, who are addicted and depressed, and I will give you rest. Marry me, for my design laws are pleasant and my workload is light."[30]

Christians know about Christ's invitation to come, but we have a hard time believing God can

---

30   Based on Matthew 11:28-30

give us contentment. The lie that salvation is transactional runs so deep that we question any Gospel that promises something for nothing. We feel that we must earn God's favor, so we focus on behavior and rules. That's why the metaphor of intimacy is so important. God doesn't want fearful compliance, shallow obedience, selfish manipulation, or sneaky last-minute conversions. These things come from fear and intimidation, which can never awaken love.

The design principles of love thrive in an atmosphere of freedom and acceptance. When these values are absent, true love shrivels and dies. Just like any devoted husband or wife, God wants intimacy, a real, honest, heart-to-heart connection. He wants our passions and our problems. He wants to walk with us when we are on top of the world and carry us through the valley of the shadow of death. God wants a dynamic relationship, not a dead, ritual-heavy, rules-based religion.

In the Bible, we witness this intimate connection of men who were close to God. Enoch's relationship is an epic model of God's design for humanity. He walked with God. Enoch did everything in the presence of God. He talked to Him throughout the day. He did chores with God. He brought God both his problems and his praises. Enoch spent so much time with God he simply walked right into heaven. We know very little about this man's life. There are no exciting stories of deliverance or temptation. The Bible's description of Enoch's life is mundane, except for two details. He walked with God, and he walked into heaven. God shows us through the quiet faithfulness of Enoch that He wants to be intimately connected to our everyday duties. God longs to be a part of the little things in life. He wants to live in our hearts and walk with us all through the day.

Abraham is another example of God's desire for humanity. In contrast to Enoch, Abraham got into a lot of trouble. Several times Abraham completely failed to trust in God when the pressure was on. Twice when a king desired his attractive wife Sarah, Abraham hid behind her skirts and lied about being her brother to save his life. Instead of being the hero and defending his woman, he let them take Sarah into their bedrooms. Abraham longed to be courageous, but he played the coward. God stepped in both times and protected Sarah. Later Abraham slept with Sarah's maidservant to help God fulfill the promise of a son. God still kept His end of the bargain even though Abraham was impatient.

This relationship was rockier than the one God enjoyed with Enoch, but God never walked away. He didn't expect Abraham to be perfect either, and He doesn't expect us to be flawless. He doesn't give up when we mess up. God comes into our fear and our pain and offers us His courage and healing. He spoke to Abraham in dreams and visions under the stars, and God even came to visit Abraham face to face. God drew near because Abraham's heart wanted Him close. This desire is the prerequisite for intimacy with God. We don't have to build up a perfect track record. We only have to want God.

Another intimate friend of God is Moses. This man also failed to follow God's guidelines. He had a quick temper, disobeyed God's direct command, and even committed murder, but beneath his fear and weakness, Moses yearned to be near God. On Mount Sinai, he had the audacity to tell God that he wanted to see Him with his own eyes. No one had seen God in His glory since Adam and Eve had sinned. What did God do? He granted Moses' request, and Moses beheld the glory of God.

For forty years, God spoke to Moses daily, and the man became a great listener. He heard God give him instructions concerning the law, the nation, the priesthood, and the tabernacle. Moses went to God for advice and wisdom, for directions and solutions. They spent so much time together that the glory of God would seep into Moses' body. When the leader stepped out of the tent after a long conversation with God, the people made Moses wear a veil over his face because it was so bright. Through Moses, we see that when we are in God's presence we learn, we change, and we glow.

Another example of God's plan for intimacy with humanity is David. This man broke so many rules that if God's law functioned like manmade, imposed law, he would be classified as a Bible villain. David lied to a priest, joined the Philistine army, pretended to be insane, failed to discipline his children, and committed adultery with a close friend's wife. Then David had that good friend killed and lied about it while he took the new widow back into his bed. Yet the Bible described him as a man after God's own heart.

Once again we see that God isn't after perfect behavior but committed hearts. David messed up big time, but he always came back to God with humility. He truly wanted to be close to God. The beautiful Psalms of David give us a peek into his spiritual diary. His songs and poems show his emotional ups and downs, yet through his words, we see that even though he failed miserably, he wanted to experience God intimately on the deepest level possible. God anointed, encouraged, trained, strengthened, elevated, and forgave David. God didn't keep all the natural consequences from harming David, but He refused to abandon His friend.

David's life shows us the dramatic contrasts of a heart connected to God. When David walks in faith, he takes down giants, defeats armies, forgives his enemies, and rules with wisdom. But when David separates himself from God, he descends into pride, adultery, and murder. His life is both a warning and an inspiration for everyone. We see the natural results of David's connection and separation played out in the beautiful and terrible consequences of his choices.

This diverse group of men all said yes to God. They heard His invitation to intimacy and walked with Him, and as they spent time with their Creator, they were transformed. They stepped into their destinies and became noble, heroic men. But they all started out just like us with a choice to connect or separate themselves from God. They doubted. They sinned. They messed up their lives. God came as close as He could to each open heart. We have the exact same opportunity. The hearts of these epic men transformed as they walked with God. Their intimate connection changed everything. God wants their experience to be ours. He wants to take our fears and give us His courage.

The Great Hunter

A long time ago, in another land, there lived another king. He too was wise and wealthy. He too had a magnificent palace with golden walls, but this king was very different from Solomon. He served a different god, a cruel god, a god who threatened and forced, a god who demanded sacrifice, and this god turned the king's heart cruel.

King Nimrod stepped off his chariot and handed the whip to his bodyguard. He looked up and up and up. The famous tower disappeared into the clouds of heaven. He smirked. They called it Nimrod's Tower, and it was a monument to his greatness, the crowning achievement of his glory, and a sure way into heaven. Marduk, his god, demanded sacrifice, and this building was a substantial sacrifice. The king marched off to the meeting. Supervisors from each level would be there to give their reports. Despite the immense height of the building and over two hundred years of construction, the king knew that the project was only half finished.

Nimrod walked up the steps that led to the first level banquet hall. As he topped the first flight of stairs, he paused to look at his city. Even though he was on the first level, he was much higher than the other buildings. He remembered the first time he had seen this valley. He had been a young man, full of dreams and pride. He remembered his brother. "What a fool," he muttered under his breath.

The Brothers

Centuries ago, Nimrod and his older brother found a good campsite after a long day hiking. The sun slipped over the far mountains as they came to the top of a rise. They stopped to catch their breath.

"Look at this valley," Nimrod whistled in awe. The brothers scanned the river as it slid along the valley and disappeared into a thick forest. "It's the perfect place for a city," he pointed. "Look. The gates could go there, and we could plant our fields over there. The river could easily supply all the water a city would need, and irrigation would be much easier than up in the hills. Plus we could use mud from the river banks to make bricks." Nimrod spoke excitedly as the great city took shape in his imagination. "We could graze our animals over there in those grassy plains and build defensive walls along that ridge."

"Brother," the older man interrupted, "What about the Call?"

Nimrod rolled his eyes. He knew about the Call. He had heard the Ancient One, his great-grandfather Noah, blabber on and on about His God and the world wide flood and the spectacular rainbow and the Call. Honestly, listening to the old stories bored him.

His older brother, Havilah, continued. "Great-grandfather told us about God's call to be fruitful and fill the earth. He also taught us to be faithful and follow the Way. Remember Noah warned us about cities. He said that before the great rains the cities were-"

Nimrod cut his brother off, "I don't care what he said. Old grandfather has lost touch with how the new world works. Living through the flood really messed him up. If it were up to Grandfather Noah, we would all live in tiny little huts around his boat and sacrifice sheep all day." Nimrod touched the bow that was slung over his shoulders. "I don't want to live that way! That life is not for me. I am a mighty hunter, and I plan on making a name for myself."

The brothers argued a little longer, but then they returned to setting up camp for the night. Lately, most of their conversations ended up in an argument. Havilah was worried about his younger brother and sensed that something deep inside

Nimrod was shifting. Nimrod no longer prayed to God with him, and he refused to sacrifice. Havilah felt Nimrod's restless rebellion simmering just below the surface. He worried a lot about Nimrod. After he bedded down for the night, he prayed silently to God for his little brother and eventually fell asleep.

But rest would not come to Nimrod, so he got up, grabbed his bow and arrows, and slipped away from camp. He walked quickly down into the lush valley, amazed by it's beauty in the moonlight. The river shimmered as he followed the winding path. Once again, Nimrod imagined his city taking shape. He envisioned massive gates and wide streets, teaming markets and lavish temples. He remembered the stories of the grand cities built before the great flood and vowed to build a city that would surpass the glory of them all.

Then, in a flash of inspiration, Nimrod saw the tower. His tower. A tower that would reach up into the heavens. His tower would be solid, able to withstand another flood. He smiled smugly envisioning all the people who would flock to him and his tower for safety. They would trust in him and what he had built, not Noah's God. Yes, building such a tall tower would be difficult, for no one had ever attempted such a feat. It would be risky and dangerous. And it would be completely rebellious. Nimrod laughed out loud, "I love it!"

The next morning, Nimrod told his brother about his plans for the tower that would touch heaven. Havilah was horrified.

"Nimrod!" he exclaimed, "You can't do this. This is blatant defiance. Not only would you be disobeying grandfather and ignoring the Call, but you would be disrespecting God Himself."

Nimrod crossed his arms defiantly. "Brother, God said to fill the earth, so I'm simply obeying by building this city and filling it with people."

"But for whose glory?" Havilah asked. "You want to build a tower so that people won't have to trust in God. Why pray? Why sacrifice? Why go to God, if you can save yourself?"

"Precisely," Nimrod said with a smirk. "Why can't we save ourselves. People like me need substance. All this faith in an invisible God is foolish. And seriously, how will killing a lamb really save me? No." Nimrod shook his head. "I need to depend on myself and what I can do. Besides, the next time there is a flood, we may not have time to build another boat. But if we have a tower, we don't have to trust in visions and dreams. We have something solid, something dependable to trust in."

Havilah's heart was breaking, and he couldn't believe the words coming out of his brother's mouth. He prayed for God's wisdom as he spoke, "God protected our grandfather during the great flood. God provided a way to save all who trusted in Him. We can trust in Him too. God is good. God loves us."

"Tell that to all the people God killed when He sent the flood," Nimrod retorted. "I don't know about this God of yours anymore. I can't see Him. I don't hear Him. And I for sure don't trust Him to save me." Nimrod thumped his chest. "I trust myself. I can save myself."

The words fell like thunderbolts. Nimrod couldn't believe that he had finally said them. Havilah plopped down as if he had been punched in the gut. He looked sick. Nimrod frowned. He knew he should take back his words. Deep down he knew they were wrong, but they felt so good. He hesitated. Havilah looked at him with tears in his eyes.

"Brother," he said in a whisper, "If you go down this path, I cannot go with you."

Nimrod stiffened. He could apologize and could say it was all a joke, and they could continue on their journey. A part of him knew what he had said wasn't true and that Havilah was right, but Nimrod was tired of living in the shadow of the ark and doing what others thought was right for him. He was tired of worship. He wanted to strike out on his own and do things his own way.

Havilah watched Nimrod closely. He had heard Noah talk about the struggle when men chose their destinies and it played out on their faces. Now he watched his own brother's battle, fervently praying for Nimrod. He knew that if Nimrod continued down the path of rebellion it would only lead to pain and suffering. He watched Nimrod's frown deepen, and a dark shadow fell across his little brother's face. Havilah read the decision so clearly, he didn't need to hear Nimrod's next words.

"It's time to say goodbye, brother."

The Tower

King Nimrod looked up into the distant hills. He could see the place where he and his brother had camped that night so very long ago. He smirked and then shook his head. Havilah had ended up living a life just like great-grandfather. He had a family. He made sacrifices. He was completely forgettable.

Nimrod, on the other hand, was the mighty hunter. People told stories of his adventures around the campfires. Nimrod was a living legend. He had drawn men to himself, and together they had conquered many people, built many cities, and become rich. Nimrod had many beautiful women and many children. He was the most powerful, the most famous, and the richest man in the entire earth. His tower was his crowning achievement. It would be remembered long after he was gone. This tower would be a symbol, a reminder, that man can pull heaven down, that man doesn't need a merciful God, that man can save himself.

King Nimrod smirked and then raised his fist to heaven shaking it defiantly. "I don't need you," he said to Havilah's God.

Suddenly he heard angry voices. Nimrod was surprised that he could hear the sounds clearly but could not understand what was being said. The king looked high up into the scaffolding and saw a work crew yelling and waving their hands in frustration. Their supervisor grabbed one of the men and shook him roughly.

Something's not right, Nimrod thought. He saw a ladder and scrambled up it. When he reached the high platform, the situation had grown worse. Other workers had surrounded the supervisor and were waving their tools threateningly at him. Nimrod felt his face turning red. He hated insubordination.

"Stand down!" the king roared. Immediately the workers recognized their ruler and dropped to their knees, their heads bowed in submission. "What's going on here?" Nimrod demanded.

The supervisor lifted his head and stammered, "I don't know what happened. One minute everyone was following my orders, and the next moment they started acting crazy. All at once they just started jabbering nonsense."

Nimrod glared at the workers. He stepped towards the man closest to him and kicked him hard. "You!" he shouted. "Get up!"

The man jumped up and looked into Nimrod's eyes. The king saw no defiance, just raw fear. The man began speaking in a strange tongue, his words rolling and jumbling together but making no sense at all. Nimrod frowned confused.

Just then the trumpet blew, and Nimrod looked up higher in the tower. Men waved alarm flags at every level. A disturbing babble of strange sounds rolled down the tower. Nimrod heard many angry voices, but he couldn't understand a single word.

"That's just it, sir," the supervisor said. "No one's speaking the same language anymore. It's all a bunch of confusion!"

But Nimrod wasn't listening; he was already sliding down the ladder. When he reached the bottom, the head architect rushed out of the tower blabbering nonsense to him. Nimrod pushed the man away. Furious nobles emerged from other doorways, frustrated workers climbed down ladders, and panicked women ran down the stairs. Soon an angry mob surrounded Nimrod, shouting and waving their fists.

Nimrod tried desperately to push his way through the crowd, but the chaos intensified. He bellowed orders. He yelled obscenities. He thundered for help. But no one obeyed, no one cared, no one understood.

Nimrod looked up at the tower's now empty scaffolds. He suddenly realized that his dream to build a tower was over. His tower would never be finished. His dream would never come true. Nimrod shook his fists at heaven and screamed. Then the babbling confusion swallowed the king.

For years and years, the half finished tower stood abandoned and alone. Its unfinished structure stood as a silent witness to man's pride and his foolish attempts to work his way to heaven. When travelers passed through the plain, they would camp in its shadow. No longer called Nimrod's Tower, everyone scoffed at the vanity, the futility, and the confusion of the Tower of Babel.[31]

Works or Worship?

King Nimrod looked at himself. King Solomon looked at God. Nimrod built a tower that promised salvation for those who worked their way to the top. Solomon built a temple that promised salvation to those who accepted the Lamb into their hearts. In the end, Nimrod's tower brought confusion, but Solomon's temple brought clarity.

The Temple of Jerusalem and the Tower of Babel. Two buildings. Two paths to eternity. Both claim to be the only way to salvation. One building calls people to work harder, to look to themselves, to earn their way to heaven. The other building reminds people that God did the hard work, that we are made to look at Him, and that the ticket to heaven is a gift. One is a monument to pride and power, while the other speaks of love and grace.

Worship

Worship is focused attention. Many people think worship is music or sermons or having devotions.

---

31   Genesis 11

But those are all outside activities. Worship happens in the heart. A believer can sing "Amazing Grace" and not worship. His mind can wander because his heart is not in it. On the outside, he looks like he worships, but on the inside, the focus is gone. Many people read their Bibles to find out what they should be doing. They create holy to-do lists and set up rules. They focus on obedience and service and keep a tally of their mistakes and failures. This is not worship either. All the focus is on self.

True worship looks at God and concentrates on Him. Worship can be singing or reading a devotional. It can happen in a church or in a field. The outward behavior can be different in different cultures with different people, but the heart looks at God, sees His goodness, and says, "I trust in You."

All of humanity has baggage left over from Nimrod's tower. We instinctively believe that if we are good enough then we will be saved. Each denomination claims to have the right set of rules and rituals, the right checklist, the magic formula. Every church preaches Christ, but those sermons come with expectations. We preach that salvation is a gift, but many, like Nimrod, work so hard to earn that gift. This is not worship; this is work.

True worship concentrates all the attention on God. Solomon's temple is full of symbols designed to strengthen our trust in God. The altar demonstrates Jesus' selfless sacrifice. The cornerstone stands for Jesus's strength under pressure. The white marble reflects Jesus' purity. The table of bread reminds us to trust in Jesus' ability to feed our souls. The lampstand shines on Jesus' light of truth. The glory hovering above the ark of the covenant declares Jesus' desire to be with us.

The more we focus on Jesus, the more we become like Him. God is too wise to be concerned with just fixing outward behavior. He wants our hearts. He wants to talk with us, walk with us, and be with us because He loves us. That's why He calls us to worship Him. It's not a call to listen to a sermon or sit in a pew. It's a call to be close to Him. That is true worship.

Worship is sitting at the feet of Jesus. It's walking with Him along the beach. It's praying with Him in the garden. It's looking up at Him on the cross. When we experience God, we will never be the same. That is why John the Baptist, a wild man with wild clothes, called the people to repent. He called them to be baptized, to get ready for the Messiah. Then, one day, John saw Him. The Baptist pointed to Jesus and told everyone how to get to heaven.

"Look! The Lamb of God who takes away the sin of the world. Look and be healed. Worship and be saved."[32]

---

32   Based on John 1:29

Main Points: I am fearless because ...

God is good.

God wants to have a relationship with me.

God's salvation is free and not earned.

God is with me.

Chapter 5

THE JUDGMENT

"I entered this world to render
judgment—to give sight to the
blind and to show those who think
they see that they are blind."[33]
—Jesus

The Faithful Husband

Hosea was a good man and a prophet. Gomer was a
beautiful woman and a prostitute. One day God told
Hosea, "Gomer is the one for you, Hosea. Marry her
and love her as I love you." God told Hosea that his
marriage would be a real life parable. Hosea would
represent God and show the people His steadfast
love and faithfulness. "It will be hard," God said.
"But you are mine, and you can do hard things."

---

33   John 9:39 NLT

Hosea had come a long way in his walk with God. He used to have such a temper and would get into fights, but years spent in the presence of God had calmed the storms of his heart. Now everyone thought of him as a gentle man.

Hosea trusted God, and he married Gomer. No one understood. Not one of his friends and certainly none of his family members, and no one supported Hosea's decision. The neighbors said he was a fool, and his parents told Hosea that Gomer would break his heart. Hosea would nod and smile, then he would remember God's words. "Love her as I love you."

The first year of their marriage was surprisingly happy. The newlyweds worked together in Hosea's shop and spent almost every moment of the day together. They went for long walks in the olive groves and talked about their childhoods, their hopes, and their fears. They laughed together often, and when she would cry, he would hold her gently.

Hosea grew to love Gomer. He admired her strength of heart and independent spirit. She was a defender of the underdog and never backed down when she confronted injustice. She loved to sing. Her beautiful voice filled his shop with light. Hosea tended to be a serious man, and Gomer's quick laughter and joyful exuberance brought balance into his life. He was a man of few words, but she hardly ever stopped talking. Hosea soon loved her fiercely. He loved her passionate heart, her tenacity in the face of obstacles, and her sensitivity for hurting people. When others looked at Gomer, they remembered a cult prostitute, but when Hosea gazed at his wife, he saw a wonderful person.

Soon Gomer was pregnant, and Hosea loved getting her the strange foods she craved, listening to her sing lullabies as she made baby clothes, and feeling the little one move and kick as his rough hand gently touched her growing belly.

When the baby came, they were overjoyed. Gomer was a devoted mother, and Hosea was a proud father. The baby boy grew quickly, and the little family settled into a new routine.

Gomer fell into depression. She became sad and distant. At first Hosea didn't notice. Then he blamed the sleepless nights as the reason for her aloofness. He was happy, and their baby was healthy. He wanted to believe that life was good.

The Longest Night

Then it happened. One night, Gomer didn't come home. Hosea was beside himself with worry. He paced back and forth holding his crying son. He imagined all sorts of terrible things that may have happened to Gomer. Had there been an accident? Had someone robbed and beaten her? Had she fallen and was not able to come home? Or was this the beginning?

Hosea begged the neighbors to watch the baby, and he frantically searched the city. He asked everyone if they had seen Gomer, but no one knew anything. Fear crept up his chest and choked him. Hosea cried out to God as he ran down deserted alleys and through dark streets searching for his lost wife.

Finally, Hosea gave up. He trudged home, put his son to bed, and waited. He sat at the table with his head in his hands. He prayed, and he worried.

Deep down, he knew what Gomer was doing, and finally he broke down and wept. Darkness enveloped him, and Hosea struggled to breathe. The pain was more than he could bear. It was the longest night of his life.

When Gomer walked in the door just before sunrise, she smelled of cheap wine and another man. Hosea felt numb. She ignored him, stumbled across the room, and flung herself into their bed.

Hosea felt his temper begin to rise. He clenched his fists and closed his eyes. Then God spoke quietly to him, "Remember. Love her as I love you." Hosea grimaced but slowly nodded and took several long, deep breaths. He released his fists and said a quick prayer. Then he stood and slowly walked toward his wife.

Gomer had been watching him, her eyes wide with fear. She knew Hosea could beat her, divorce her, and kick her out. Gomer sat up and lifted her chin, trying to look calm, but her eyes showed terror. Hosea knelt before her and looked at his wife. He remembered all their good times, the happy memories, and intimate moments, her sweet laughter and soft lullabies. Tears glistened in his eyes. He was normally not emotional, Gomer was surprised at his tenderness.

"I will love you forever," he promised.

Abandoned

Nine months later, when she had her second baby, no one, not even Hosea, believed the baby girl was his. But it didn't matter to Hosea. He loved the little bundle with all his heart. Gomer seemed to settle back into the rhythm of the house. She cared for the children and still helped Hosea in the shop. She even began to sing again.

Three months later, Gomer left again. This time she didn't come back for days. Hosea was alone with the babies, and people started to talk. It was hard for the man of God. Hosea had done everything right. He loved Gomer, accepted her, and had even forgiven her, but she was faithless. The emotions that swirled in Hosea's heart threatened to overwhelm him as he struggled with betrayal, despair, rage, and love. He kept hearing God tell him to love her, but he didn't know how he would respond when she returned. He prayed all through the day, and sometimes all night long as he lay awake in his bed all alone. Slowly God soothed his turbulent heart and filled him with a peace that even Hoesa could not understand.

Months and months went by. Hosea finally figured out how to run his shop, manage a toddler, and care for the baby all at the same time. When Gomer limped through the front door, she had a black eye and a busted lip. Her clothes were torn and dirty, and her once-gorgeous hair was gone. Bald, bleeding, and broken, Gomer could barely stand. She leaned against the door post. Instead of righteous anger, Hosea felt only heartbroken sympathy. Gomer looked so miserable, so sad. She didn't apologize. She just hung her head in shame. Hosea took her hand and led her to a chair. Then he quickly poured a basin of water and began to dab at her cuts.

He was silent for a long time, but then she looked at him. As their eyes met, Hosea felt her pain and her shame. He hoped she could feel his love and his acceptance. Hosea leaned forward and touched his forehead to hers.

"I will love you forever," he said. Gomer tucked her face into his shoulder and sobbed. Hosea held her for a long time.

The Heartbreak Years

Altogether Gomer and Hosea had three children, but they all looked so different, none of the neighbors believed the prophet had fathered any of them. Hosea heard the gossip as he walked in the marketplace. No one could understand why such a noble man wasted his love on such a loose woman. His family and friends agreed that Hosea should divorce Gomer and find a better wife who would bring him honor and joy rather than disgrace and pain. But Hosea refused to abandon his unfaithful wife.

Despite Hosea's loyalty, over time the affairs became less and less discreet. Many times Gomer would be gone from home for months at a time, yet somehow Hosea managed.

At first, Gomer was confused by Hosea's unconditional love. No man had ever treated her with kind respect, but soon her bewilderment soured into contempt. She looked down on his simple faith and small business. Hosea was not exciting like the other men she enjoyed. She criticized her husband and put him down in front of the children. She mocked him as he led the family in worship and flew into rages when he gently asked for her help with the children. Gomer bragged about her lovers and flaunted the nice things they bought her, things Hosea could never afford. Yet his answer was always the same, "I will love you forever."

Gone

Then one day, Gomer left for good. She took a few of her things and simply walked out the door. She didn't kiss her children or tell Hosea where she was going. She simply vanished. Soon rumors trickled back that she was living with one of the nobles as his concubine. People whispered that she drank out of silver goblets and wore Egyptian linen. These words stung Hosea's broken heart, but he remembered God's words, "Love her as I love you."

When Hosea saw Gomer's rebelliousness, he remembered his sins. He remembered his fiery temper and the many fights of his youth. Hosea had been cruel and violent, yet God had gently molded his character. The divine forgiveness, grace, and acceptance softened Hosea's stony heart, and over time the man with the temper became a prophet of God. Hosea couldn't hate Gomer even though her adultery cut deep into his soul.

Through his incredible pain, Hosea finally began to understand God's love. The stunning beauty of God's faithfulness and forgiveness left Hosea in awe. He saw God's faithfulness so clearly as he lived through the stressful days and lonely nights. His prayers became as natural as breathing as He asked God for patience with his children, wisdom in his business, courage in his ministry, and comfort in the darkness. His prayer life was so vibrant that some days, people said his face glowed. When Hosea spoke of God's faithfulness, people listened.

The Auction

Two years passed. The children stopped asking for their mother, and Hosea found a new routine. The pain had slowly numbed, but he still missed her warm laughter and cheerful songs. One day as he walked through the marketplace, he saw her standing on the slaver's block.

"Gomer," he gasped as his heart jumped into his throat.

She was naked, striped bare, and exposed to everyone in the crowd. The seductive curve of her youthful body had disappeared. Now Gomer was thin and sickly. Her ribs stuck out, and her skinny legs were caked with blood and dirt. Her hair was streaked with gray and filth, and her face was swollen from beatings. Gomer's shoulders slumped in despair, and she stared at the ground. The light that used to dance in her eyes had vanished.

Hosea quickly walked toward her. Pure rage filled his heart, not at Gomer, but at the monster responsible for her abuse. He pushed his way through the crowd until he was standing right in front of Gomer. Hosea's heart pounded in his chest and his jaw twitched.

A nobleman with yellow teeth and an embroidered cloak laughed and made a crude joke. "I've heard about this one," he said with a dirty look. "She doesn't look too good, but I hear she can-"

Hosea raised his hand and called out a bid. The noble countered. Without thinking, Hosea raised the bid. Soon the two men were locked in a bidding war. The price went much higher than a woman in Gomer's condition deserved. One man bid for his pride, and the other fought for his wife.

"Twenty shekels!" the noble shouted, and the crowd gasped. Hosea was shocked. He closed his eyes and tried to do some calculations, but all he could hear was God's calm voice. "Love her as I love you."

The evening trumpet echoed from the temple, and Hosea thought of the sacrifice. He thought of the Messiah and the price He would pay. Hosea had fifteen shekels in his pouch and the sack of barley that was supposed to last the family for the rest of the year. *That means I have thirty shekels,* Hosea thought. *That's more than I make in a year.* He looked at Gomer. *She's worth it,* he decided. Hosea clenched his fists.

"Thirty shekels for my wife!" he said. It was everything he had.

Stunned silence filled the marketplace. The crowd stared at Hosea. The slaver's mouth gaped wide in disbelief. The noble glared at Hosea. "She's not worth that much. You may be the prophet, but you are a fool!" He stomped off muttering under his breath.

"Sold!" A hammer slammed down, and soon a man roughly pushed Gomer toward Hosea. He quickly threw his cloak around her bruised shoulders. Gomer could barely walk, so Hosea scooped her up in his arms and carried her home.

Later that night, Hosea wiped Gomer's feverish brow. He bathed her broken body and put ointment on her wounds. Every time she winced in pain, his heart shuddered. He poured oil on Gomer's hair and softly combed out the tangles. He tucked her into their bed and brought her soup. He silently fed her with a spoon and dabbed her mouth with a soft cloth.

The whole time she didn't look at him. She just gazed at the wall. The children were with a friendly neighbor for the night, so it was just the two of them.

Gomer was silent. She was a broken shell of the vivacious girl Hosea had married years ago.

Hosea took a deep breath and spoke. "I bought you, but you are not my slave. You are my wife, and you are free. If you want to leave when you are healthy, that is your choice." Hosea paused and waited for Gomer to respond, but she said nothing. He took a deep breath and continued, "If you decide to stay, there are expectations. You must never commit adultery again. You must be faithful to me. I promise to be faithful to you."

She turned her head and stared at the wall. Hosea was silent for a long time. He saw her broken body and felt her shattered soul. He was overcome with compassion for Gomer. Her terrible choices had destroyed her, but Hosea loved Gomer too much to control her. If she chose to stay, he would love her with all his heart, but if she decided to leave again, he would let her go. It would break his heart, but he would not force her to love him. The choice was hers.

Hosea leaned over and kissed her forehead. "I love you forever."[34]

God's Love

God put this love story right in the middle of the Bible. He wants intimacy with us for so many reasons. He knows this is the only experience that will completely ennoble us, mature us, and fulfill us. He made fish to swim, birds to fly, and humans to love. When we love God above everything else, then we step into our purpose and truly live. God has done everything He can to win our love and trust. God washed dirty feet and freed rebellious slaves. God provided manna in the desert and walked in the fiery furnace. God made a promise to Adam and fulfilled it on the cross. God loves us. We were custom-made for His love.

The Judgment is our response to God. When we accept His invitation to intimacy, we will experience deep levels of peace and joy. Like all relationships, there will be ups and downs, but when we commit to spiritual intimacy, when we marry God in our hearts, when we become one with our Savior, we finally find what we were looking for. Unfortunately, many people see the Judgment very differently.

---

34   The book of Hosea

A Bad Joke

Knock, Knock.
Who's there?
Jesus. Let me in.
Why?
So I can save you.
From what?
From what I'll do to you if you don't let me in.[35]

Judgment Day. It scares even the best of Christians. Many of us were brought up with stories of a great heavenly courtroom where God the Father glares down at us from a giant podium. Satan is our accuser, and Jesus is our defense attorney. They battle it out before God. Satan points to every flaw, every sinful mistake, every willful act of defiance. Jesus points to His nail-pierced hands, reminds the Father that He paid the price with His blood, and pleads for mercy.

For many, this is how they view salvation. They see God as the great Punisher of sin. They come to Jesus to be covered in His blood so that they can be saved from God's wrath. They come to Jesus because they are afraid of punishment.

These frightened believers think the final, eternal decision belongs to someone else. God the Father is the Great Judge who decides if we are good enough, if all our sins are confessed so they can be

---

35 Multiple Internet locations with original source unknown.

forgiven, and if we truly deserve to be in heaven. Then the Judge makes the call. Some are relieved when they hear God's judgment and are welcomed into heavenly bliss, while the vast majority of others crumple to the floor in despair, knowing that God is sending them straight to hell to be tortured in the fire of His divine wrath.

This view of the judgment and hell is terrifying and pagan. Stories of an angry god harshly judging humanity and then punishing them by sending them to torment is found in the hieroglyphics of Egypt, in the temples of Greece and Rome, and in the oral traditions of the wild tribes of the north. But this idea is strangely absent in the teachings of Jesus. He gives us hints about the judgment in parables, but He is the most clear in a midnight conversation with Nichodemus. It's the conversation that holds the most famous verse in the Bible, John 3:16.

In this conversation with one of Israel's greatest teachers, Jesus explains the truth about the judgment. It's very simple. There are no lawyers or judges or juries. There are three simple decisions. The first one was made by God. The second is made by individuals. The last one is God's acceptance of that choice.

The First Judgment

John 3:16 says God loved the whole world so much that He gave His Son. This first Judgment Day took place long ago when God decided that He would give His Son to rescue us. Before Adam and Eve sinned, Jesus decided that He would leave heaven and die for humanity. The first judgment is when God looked at all of us and said, "You are worth it. You are valuable." God judged everyone, and then said we were worth dying for.

The Second Judgment

The second judgment is our response to this gift. John 3:16 goes on to say, "Whoever believes may have eternal life." God offers eternal life to everyone. He doesn't play favorites. He is willing to heal all of us. The second judgment is our decision to accept the healing and see the light or turn away and remain in the darkness.

It is time to wake up and realize that Jesus stands at the door of our hearts and knocks.[36] He knows that sin is killing us, and He is ready to heal us. He bought the remedy with His blood on the cross, and He is eager to give it to us.

Will we let Him in? Can we give Him our hearts, our lives, our dreams, our destiny? Our answer and our eternity depends on how we view God's character.

Jesus came to prove that God is trustworthy, faithful, and loving. His death on the cross opened the way to salvation healing. In John 14:9, Jesus told

---

36 Revelation 3:20

His disciples, "Anyone who has seen Me has seen the Father." Then in John 17:6, Jesus prayed to His Father and said, "I have made You known to the ones you gave me."

Jesus showed us in every interaction that God is trustworthy. When He healed the sick, praised the faith of the Centurion, and brought a little girl back to life, Jesus showed us His heart. When He spoke to the lepers outside a village, the Pharisees in the temple, or the little children on His knees, Jesus showed us His goodness. Jesus proved that God always has the best intentions for us. God will never double cross us or take advantage of us. God will never use His divine power to control us or hurt us.

Jesus came to answer the question in every heart. *Can I really trust God?*

His entire life was a resounding, "Yes!"

This second Judgment Day is like Christmas morning. The kids wake up early and bound down the stairs. Mom and Dad are standing by the tree with big smiles on their faces and brightly wrapped packages piled around their slippers. The kids careen into the room and suddenly stop. Their little heads swivel from their parents to the gifts. Now they decide. Do they open the gifts or leave them under the tree?

No kids stomp out of the room and head to the kitchen for a stale Pop-Tart. Every single kid on the planet dives into the presents and tears them open.

That's what Jesus meant when He said that we must become like little children.

Judgment Day is better than Christmas morning. We bound into the room and stop. God stands next to another tree, but this one has no decorations, just a few nails. Beneath it we find another present, but this present is not wrapped. It doesn't have any bows. This present is God Himself. Then He smiles and holds out His nail-scarred hands. We look at the cross and then at Jesus, our Immanuel.

Now we decide.

Do we run into His arms? Do we say yes to the light? Or do we turn our backs on Him and walk away from His Presence into the stale, black darkness?

The second judgment is our call, but Jesus's grace is persistent. Jesus doesn't give up easily. He warned Peter about his pride. He washed Judas' feet before the betrayal. He performed miracles in front of the Pharisees. He sat on a donkey and looked out at Jerusalem and wept. He cried, "O Jerusalem, how I longed to gather you into My arms. I sent you prophets. I gave you the Scriptures. I even came in person. I taught in your temple. I healed in your streets. But you would not have me."[37] What more could He have done?

---

37   Based on multiple translations of Matthew 23:37

The Third Judgment

The third judgment is when Jesus accepts our final decisions. John 3:18 promises that people who choose to believe will be saved, but warns that those who choose not to believe will be condemned. The choice is ours, and God respects our judgment of Him. God warmly welcomes those who trust and accept Him, but Jesus sadly lets go of those who have rejected Him. Jesus explained the judgment clearly when He said, "This is the judgment. Light has come into the world, but men loved darkness. Everyone who does evil hates the light and will not come into the light."[38] It is our choice to either come into the light or remain in darkness. Whoever chooses not to believe is lost.[39] The final judgment is when God respects the freedom of every soul and gives us what we want.

While there is still time, Jesus relentlessly pursues us with His love, but there comes a point where Jesus will acknowledge the rejection as our ultimate choice. The Bible calls it the unpardonable sin. He will never force Himself on anyone. The third Judgment Day is not when God decides if we are good enough for Him. It's when He accepts our final judgment of Him.

---

38   Based on multiple translations of John 3:19-20

39   John 3:18

The Invitation

Once upon a time, a man sent out invitations to his wedding feast. This man was very wealthy, and he wanted to put on a party with so much food, wine, and entertainment that it would be remembered for generations. He would shower his friends, family members, and guests with lavish gifts. So he hired the best musicians, the most talented dancers, the most famous chefs. But this man had an enemy, a former servant who was jealous and hated him.

When the Bridegroom sent out the invitations, the evil servant spread lies. The enemy claimed that the Bridegroom was planning to get his guests drunk and then sell them all as slaves. He accused the host of setting up a trap to kidnap the women and force them into his secret harem. The enemy whispered that the wine was poisoned so the Bridegroom could watch his guests writhe in agony and die at his home.

Everyone invited had dealt with the Bridegroom before. He had traded with them at the marketplace. He had shared his grain when there had been a famine. He had hired their sons when they needed work. He had always been fair and kind and just. But they wondered at his wealth. The evil servant suggested that this wealth had been gained through fraud and theft, and this party was the final stage of a mastermind plot to take over the entire kingdom and set himself up as a dictator.

Some believed the lies. Others cared too much about what their neighbors thought of them. Many pretended to be too busy. And one by one every neighbor, family member, and friend threw away their invitation.

When the day of his wedding arrived, no one came. No one was there to celebrate with the Bride and Bridegroom. No one enjoyed the exquisite food, the vintage wine, or the expensive gifts. They missed out on sharing the Bridegroom's joy.

The evil servant laughed at the extravagant waste. He believed that the outrageous bill would ruin the Bridegroom's finances, but the Host did a strange thing. When no one came to the party, He sent out more invitations. This time he invited everyone, not just his neighbors and the nobles. He invited beggars and slaves. He invited foreigners and fishermen. He invited prostitutes and tax collectors. He invited shepherds and soldiers.

And these people came.

They walked into the banquet hall with their mouths wide open. The Bridegroom met each guest and welcomed them with a warm smile. He showered them with new robes and crowns of gold. He served them hors d'oeuvres and wine with his own hand. He laughed at their jokes and slapped them on the back. He completely enjoyed himself, and everyone there felt his genuine love.

When the time came for the wedding, there were no strangers, just a room full of good friends. When he kissed his bride, the hall erupted into cheers.

Word of the Bridegroom's wedding spread far and wide. Soon everyone knew about his generosity, kindness, and hospitality. Merchants and traders came to do business with the host who had such a sterling reputation. Kings sent envoys to congratulate the Bridegroom and invite him and his bride to their lands. Instead of being a catastrophe, the feast was a catalyst that launched the generous host into higher levels of success.

Those who believed the enemy's lies and rejected the invitation regretted their decision for the rest of their lives. But every person who accepted the gracious Host's invitation spoke of that celebration with warm memories.

The wedding feast was a judgment, not of the quality of the guests, but of the character of the host. People refused to come because they judged the Bridegroom as untrustworthy. Other people came because they were willing to trust the Bridegroom. The party was open to everyone who would come. The judgment was in the hands of those that opened the invitation.[40]

---

40   Matthew 22:1-14, Luke 14:15-24

Who Is the Judge?

All three judgments are hidden in this parable. The first judgment is in the invitations. The Bridegroom invited everyone. No one earned an invitation. No one had to buy a ticket to get into the party. The feast was a free gift. Then people either declined or accepted. This is the second judgment. The people judged the Bridegroom. Each person had his or her reasons for their decision, but it was their call. They decided to come to the party or stay at home. The final judgment almost slips past us. The Bridegroom stands at his door and welcomes everyone who walks in. He gives them gifts, serves them food, and enjoys their company. He turns no one away. He accepted their acceptance. But what about everyone who rejected the Bridegroom? Did he send out his servants to force them to come to the wedding? No. He accepted their rejection. He went ahead and got married without them. This is the Judgment.

Jesus died on the cross for everyone and invites us all to heaven. Some will gladly accept the invitation, and others will sadly reject it. Jesus accepts our final choice. It's our decision. It's our judgment.

The Conspiracy

"It's judgment day," the priest spat. "When the governor brings out the two men, he will give us a choice. Barabbas must be set free. Jesus must die."

The men nodded and held out their hands for the money. The priest rolled his eyes. "How slow are you?" he exclaimed. "Didn't you hear anything I just said? This man, this false Messiah, Jesus, is a deceiver and full of demons! It is our duty to free the nation of this monster."

One of the men stepped closer to the priest. He pushed back a dirty, red turban. "We don't care about your conspiracies. We just want your coins. Pay up like you promised, or we are going back to the tavern."

The priest glared at the men. He shoved his hand into his belt and brought out some silver. He dropped the coins into filthy palms and recoiled. He had paid Judas earlier; now he was paying these slum thugs. These were the kind of men who followed Jesus—greedy, dirty, uneducated fools. How fitting that these would be the men who would send the blasphemer to the cross.

The priest smiled wickedly. "Now that you have your money, you will do exactly as I said."

"Don't worry about a thing," another man grinned. "We know how to raise a ruckus." The men dispersed and began to agitate the crowd.

The priest turned with a smug look across his face. He walked toward a group of shifty-looking men and gave the same instructions.

"Hey," a voice interrupted. "What is happening here?" The priest saw a man carrying a basket of bread. "I was on my way to the market and heard that there was money to be made near Pilate's hall."

"Yes," the priest said and quickly explained the situation. "Remember, when Pilate offers us Jesus, we all shout, 'Crucify him!'"

The man was horrified. "Are you talking about Jesus of Nazareth?"

"Of course, I am!" The priest paid the men quickly and then disappeared into the crowd.

The man stood in shock. How could this be? Then he remembered the first day he had seen Jesus.

The Mud

The day began in darkness, just like every other day of his life. Aaron sat on a cold stone step and held out a small cup. He shook it so the coins inside jingled. He could hear the market waking up. A cow bawled. The baker yelled at his boy again. Someone dropped a basket of figs.

Aaron called out, "Coins! Coins for a blind man! God will see your goodness and reward you."

Someone dropped a coin into his cup. "Thank you, kind soul," he called out as the footsteps faded.

The morning was unusual. The baker gave him a small, warm loaf of bread, but he didn't take out a coin from the cup this time. The gruff man mumbled something about loving his neighbors.

Aaron smiled. *Today was going to be a good day,* he decided.

Toward late afternoon, a group of men walked past him. They were speaking about religious matters, and Aaron knew they wouldn't give him any coins. He guessed they were Pharisees and hoped they would move along quickly. Last week, a Pharisee had stopped right next to him and had prayed out loud for what seemed like eternity. Not only was the prayer painfully long and dull, but no one gave Aaron money when the Pharisees were around because inevitably the holy men would begin to preach about how charity should be donated to the temple instead of to beggars.

The group of men stopped in front of Aaron. He shifted his weight on the hard step and inwardly groaned.

"Teacher," one of the men spoke. "Do you see this blindman?"

I'm right here, Aaron thought. *I'm blind not deaf.*

The man continued to speak. "Whose sin caused his blindness? Is it his parents' fault or his?"

Aaron hung his head, the old shame haunting him again. It was hard enough being blind, but he hated hearing the harsh judgments. Everyone blamed his parents or whispered about a secret sin he must have committed. It wasn't fair.

"Neither!" a new voice shot into his darkness. "This blindness is not the result of this man's sins or the sins of his parents."

Aaron sat up straighter.

The voice continued. "This happened so that the power of God could be seen in him."

Chills ran down Aaron's arms. He expected more accusations about his hidden sins, but this Teacher started talking about the power of God. The Man's words were different. It wasn't just talk. Aaron could feel something powerful in this Teacher's words. He had heard rumors about a prophet named Jesus who could work miracles. He was afraid to hope, but something in his heart thrilled at the thought that maybe the Prophet was standing next to him.

"As long as it is day, we must do the work of Him who sent Me," the voice spoke again. "Night is coming when no one can work." Aaron heard someone crouch next to him, and the familiar voice said, "While I am in the world, I am the Light of the world."

Then Aaron heard someone spit in the dirt near his feet and crouch down next to him. Someone murmured, "What is Jesus doing?" Aaron gasped and tipped his head to the side, straining to hear what was happening. His heart pounded, and his breathing was shallow.

Then the voice spoke again, but this time it was much closer and carried a soft warmth. "Don't be afraid. I am going to touch your eyes."

Aaron felt something warm and wet and gritty being smeared over his closed eyes. Then strong hands lifted him up. Aaron stood on shaky legs. He instinctively reached for his staff, and someone put it into his hands.

Someone was standing next to him. Aaron could smell Him. It wasn't a perfumed Pharisee like he expected. It was a common man who smelled like sweat and the marketplace. The Man standing next to Aaron spoke with a smile. "Go and wash in the pool of Siloam." Aaron felt a gentle pat on his back, and then he was alone.

Aaron started walking in the direction of the pool. It was an easy walk from his familiar step up a long street and down some stairs. When he arrived at the pool, he asked a stranger to help him get to the water. A kind, old woman took his hand in hers and led him to a place where he could sit next to the pool.

Aaron dipped his hands into the water and brought it to his face. He splashed the water and rubbed his eyes. He blinked and then he cried out.

Sunlight danced across the water. He stared down at his wet hands and watched the droplets fall and splash into the pool. Powerful emotions swept through his body, and Aaron began to shake with joy and disbelief. Tears blurred his new vision, but he quickly wiped them away. He turned ecstatically toward the person closest to him and looked into the wrinkled face of the kind woman who had helped him. Her eyes were wide, and her mouth was open in disbelief. She was beautiful.

"I can see! I can see!" Aaron yelled. He jumped up and threw his hands into the air. "Praise the Lord! I can see!"

The Interrogation

Later that day, Aaron stood between two burly guards. He had been arrested and was waiting to be questioned by the judges, but he couldn't stop smiling.

He grinned and leaned over to one of the guards. "I can see," he said excitedly.

"I know," the guard grunted. "That's why you're here."

Aaron looked up and around, then side to side, taking in as much as he could see. "This place is magnificent. Can you believe how large these columns are?"

The guards ignored him.

Two massive doors opened, and a scribe scurried out and motioned for Aaron to enter. Aaron walked in gazing at the room with its vaulted ceiling and marble benches. Dozens of men clothed in rich robes with intricate embroidery sat with scowls on their faces. Aaron knew he should be intimidated, but he didn't care. He could see!

A man with a long white beard cleared his throat and began the examination. It started with mundae questions about his name, his parents, his home.

Aaron answered the questions, all the while craning his neck around to drink in every detail he could see.

Then a younger man snapped at Aaron. "Are you the blindman who sits on the steps near the market?"

Aaron recognized the voice. It was the long-winded man of prayer. Aaron examined the man more closely and nodded his head. *Yes,* he thought, *This man looks just like he sounds.*

"Answer me!" the man shouted.

Aaron jumped. "Yes, sir. I am the blindman … er … No, I mean I was the blindman. But now I can see, just like you." He laughed, but as he quickly scanned the room, his laughter faded away. *Why is everyone so angry here?* he wondered.

"Now tell us how you were healed," the older man with the beard ordered.

"Oh, I'd love to," Aaron said, and then he launched into his story. He skipped the part about being annoyed with Pharisees who prayed too long, because he didn't think that detail was very important, but he covered everything else. When he finished his story, he stopped and waited for someone to smile or congratulate him or at least praise the Lord, but he was met only with cold indifference and scornful stares.

"Do you know what day it is?" another priest shot the question as if it was an accusation.

Aaron frowned and thought for a moment. He was so excited about being able to see that he had no idea.

"It's the Sabbath!" the priest growled. "You are a Sabbath breaker!"

Aaron couldn't believe his ears. "What?" he said incredulously. "How am I breaking the Sabbath?"

The younger priest, the one who loved long prayers, jumped out of his seat and tore into Aaron. "You are a disturbance in the temple praising God at the top of your lungs. You bathed in a public pool on the Sabbath, and worse still, you are giving credit to a sinner who breaks the Sabbath by performing miracles and then commands people to do work on God's holy day!"

Aaron was incredulous. He didn't know what to say.

A different rabbi spoke up. "How can a man who performs such wonders be a sinner?"

Aaron looked and saw a friendly face. This man was also older, but his gray beard was short, and his eyes were kind.

"Nicodemus," the younger priest groaned. "Why do you always defend this false teacher?"

"I only speak what I believe is right according to our Scriptures and traditions." Nicodemus stood to speak, but was cut off by another priest. Soon the entire council was in an uproar. Some men were shouting and shaking their fists, while others waved their hands in the air and shook their heads. Aaron thought the whole ordeal was almost funny.

Finally, the older priest with the long beard stood. Everyone noticed, and soon the room was quiet again. The old priest scowled at Aaron.

"What about you, young man?" the priest said hoarsely. "What do you say about Him, since He opened your eyes?"

Aaron spoke straight from his heart, without thinking, but with deep conviction. "He is a prophet."

The Son of Man

The sun had already set when Aaron walked out of the temple in a daze. He was thrilled that he could see, but he was crushed because now he could never enter the temple again. The priests had judged him as unworthy and excommunicated him forever. He had entered the judgment hall expecting everyone to rejoice with him and praise God, but he left the room confused and heartbroken. They had insulted his parents, condemned the Man who healed him, and called Aaron the worst of sinners. Now he felt lost and alone.

"What do I do now?" Aaron said to no one.

"You can believe," a voice answered.

Aaron's heart skipped a beat. He recognized that voice. Aaron turned around and saw a Man.

The Man spoke, "Do you believe in the Son of Man?"

Aaron knew that the Son of Man was another name for the Messiah. "Who is He, sir?" Aaron stepped forward and looked deeply into the man's eyes. "Tell me so that I may believe in Him."

The Man held Aaron's gaze. Aaron knew that this was the one who had healed him, but he wasn't sure if the person standing in front of him was the Messiah. The Man's eyes were deep and kind. Aaron felt the peace coming from the Man's presence.

The Man's face broke out into a warm smile. "You have seen Him; in fact, He is the one speaking with you right now."

Aaron fell to his knees. "Lord," he said, "I believe." Aaron touched his head to the ground and worshipped at the feet of the Messiah, his Healer. Tears streamed down Aaron's face as he whispered, "Thank you. Thank you. Thank you." His heart was full of love, and his world was finally full of light.

Then someone cleared his throat loudly and coughed. Aaron sat up and looked around. A group of priests stood frowning, their arms crossed and their lips curled in disgust. Aaron felt a cold darkness creep into his heart.

The Messiah moved and stood in between the priests and Aaron.

"We have judged this man as a sinner and have thrown him out of the temple." A priest spit onto the ground near Aaron.

"I entered this world to give the true judgment," the Messiah said strongly. "To give sight to the blind and to show those who think they can see that they are blind."

"What!?" a priest scoffed. "Are you accusing us of being blind?" The group grumbled, and Aaron felt the darkness surge in power.

The Messiah took a step closer, and the darkness recoiled. "If you were truly blind, then you would not be guilty. But because you claim to see the truth and yet walk in darkness, your blindness cannot be healed."

Aaron watched the priest shake their robes in disgust and stride back into the temple. The Messiah sadly shook his head. "Oh, that you would turn to Me and be healed," He said quietly. "Then you would truly see."[41]

The Sentence

Just then, someone in the courtyard stomped on Aaron' foot, snapping him back to the present. His daydream of Jesus vanished and was replaced by the surly mob.

"Look! Here they come!" someone pointed.

The governor emerged from the shadows and sat down. Then soldiers led two men out and stood them on either side of the great judgment seat. One man glared at the crowd defiantly. He looked like a hard criminal.

"Barabbas," Aaron heard one man say. "I've heard that he's killed six men in cold blood."

---

41   John 9

Then Aaron looked at Jesus. Even from far away, Aaron could sense the same healing presence he'd experienced the day he first met Jesus. In the sea of turmoil, Jesus exuded strength and dignity and light.

The governor said something, but Aaron couldn't hear him. He was looking at Jesus. Aaron's eyes drank in every detail. He saw Jesus's calm face, the hands tied behind His back, the dried blood at the side of His mouth. *What was Jesus doing up there?* Aaron wondered. This man was the Messiah, not a criminal. Something was very wrong.

Then the crowd erupted. "Give us Barabbas!" they chanted. "Give us Barabbas!"

Aaron was shocked. Was the crowd asking for Barabbas' release? Then he understood.

He shouted, "Jesus! Give us Jesus!" He shouted over and over, but the other chant grew stronger and drowned out his voice. Aaron shoved his way forward, screaming at the top of his lungs, "Give us Jesus! Give us Jesus!"

The governor held up his hands for silence. The mob fell quiet, but Aaron felt an icy darkness flowing through the people. He remembered the cold feeling the day the Messiah had stood in front of the priests and teachers, but today the darkness was larger, stronger, and deeper. Men with wild eyes and teeth bared surrounded Aaron. *Were they possessed by demons?* he shuddered. Chills ran down Aaron's spine. Then he looked back at Jesus and saw the same calm strength. He pushed forward, trying to reach Jesus, trying to get closer.

"What about your king?" The governor said pointing to Jesus. "What shall I do with Jesus of Nazareth?" His question echoed against the walls of the courtyard, and for one moment, there was silence.

Aaron opened his mouth to shout, but then a wave of evil engulfed him.

"Crucify him! Crucify him!"

"No!" Aaron cried. "Have mercy on the Son of David! Have mercy!"

He struggled to move forward. "Let Him go! He healed me! He healed me!"

A large man in a red turban grabbed Aaron. "Shut your mouth, or I'll do it for you." He shoved Aaron hard.

Aaron looked over the red turban and at Jesus. Their eyes met. The world froze. The crowd and their shouts faded. All Aaron could see was Jesus' noble face. Aaron reached out his hand as if to wipe the blood away from Jesus' eyes. Jesus gazed directly at Aaron. Jesus didn't speak, but Aaron felt something.

He felt like the healing of his eyes was just the beginning. Jesus had come to battle the darkness of the world and give light not just to him, but to everyone. He felt a pulse of love, and he knew that he could not stop what was going to happen.

The moment passed as quickly as it began, and someone stepped between Jesus and Aaron. He shook his head and looked around. Men shouted and waved their fists in the air. Someone screamed, "We have no king but Caesar!" Evil was present; Aaron could taste it.

Why can't they see? he wondered. *Jesus never hurt anyone. He just healed and helped people. He healed me and now I see. How can they be so blind?*

The crowd became silent again. Aaron turned and heard the governor say, "Why? What crime has he committed?"

Then the shouting and cursing rose with even more fury. Something inside Aaron surged upward. His chest lifted, and he remembered Jesus' words, "While I am in the world, I am the Light of the world."

Then Aaron grabbed the man next to him. "Jesus healed me!" he shouted. "This man gave me my sight!"

The man stopped shouting and looked at him.

"He healed me!"

Another man lowered his fist and looked at Aaron. Then the big man with the red turban emerged from the mob. He grabbed the front of Aaron's tunic and lifted him off the ground with a huge fist.

"It looks like I'm going to have to shut you up." His breath reeked of onions and barley beer. Then he raised his other fist and smashed it into Aaron' face.

Everything went black.[42]

---

42   Matthew 27

The Darkness

Hours later, when Aaron opened his eyes, all he could see was darkness. For a moment, he panicked and believed that he was blind again, but then the courtyard came into focus. It was dark, but he could see the stones and pieces of rubbish scattered across the ground. His head throbbed.

A wet cloth touched his forehead. A gentle voice spoke in the darkness. "Are you hurt badly?"

"Where did they take Him?" Aaron said as he tried to sit up. Pain shot through his jaw.

"They took him to Skull Rock." The voice was sad. "He's on a cross right now. I couldn't watch any longer."

Tears welled up and rolled down Aaron's cheeks.

"If I am lifted up, I will draw all men toward me," the man said. He sighed. "He told me that a long time ago."

Aaron looked at the man. It was hard to see in the dark, but he looked like a priest.

"Aren't you one of those priests who was paying people to shout for Barabbas?" Aaron asked.

"No," the other man shook his head slowly. "Those men hate Jesus, but I love Him. I met Him once." Then Nichodemus told Aaron about a conversation he had with Jesus in the middle of the night years ago.

"Jesus said God loved the world so much that He gave His very Son, so that anyone who believes will not die but have eternal life." The old man paused. "I didn't understand what He meant until today. He also said that He came into this world to save it, not to judge it, and that if He was lifted up, then He would draw all men to Himself."

Nichodemus continued, "I've been teaching my whole life that Judgment Day is when God will look at us and weigh our good deeds against our bad deeds. I've told many people that if they aren't good enough, God will send them away."

Aaron nodded. He had heard the rabbis' teachings. He had always dreaded Judgment Day because he knew he would never be good enough for God. Then he met Jesus.

"He told me that He came to this world for judgment." Aaron remembered Jesus's words. "Then He said that he would give sight to the blind but not to those who claim to see."

The old priest looked at Aaron. "You seem confused, my friend," Nichodemus said. "I remember being confused myself, but now it makes perfect sense. Jesus told me that the Light has come into the darkness, but men loved the darkness. That's what happened today." The old man's voice cracked. "Our nation chose to remain blind. It was our Judgment Day. We weren't being judged; He was. We judged Him as unworthy. We pushed Him away. We wouldn't let Him heal us." Then Nichodemus put his head in his hands and sobs shook his body.[43]

---

43   John 3

Aaron reached out and put his arm around the priest. "Jesus healed me. I was blind, but now I see because of Him. I'm not a good man, and I know my bad deeds weigh more than my good ones, but when I saw His face, none of that mattered." Aaron swallowed hard. "I wasn't afraid of the judgment after meeting Jesus. He opened the eyes of my soul and let the light in. I just want to see Him again. It seems so dark, now that He's gone."

The old rabbi had stopped crying and sniffed, "Yes, but we can still honor Him." Nichodemus slowly stood up. "Do you want to see Him one last time?" He held out his hand.

Aaron reached out, and the old man helped him stand. "More than anything," he said.

"Good." Nichodemus started walking. "I must go to Pilate and call in a favor. Then I will need your help."

The two men walked out of the dark courtyard and disappeared into the shadows of the city. Even though it was the middle of the day, darkness was everywhere. The light had gone out. The darkness had won for now.[44]

Sunrise

The wet grass felt cold in the early morning mist. Aaron looked up at the last stars in the sky. The darkness slowly gave way to the light as the sun rose

---

44   John 19:38-42

over the Judean hills and turned the edges of the dark blue clouds brilliant orange. It was beautiful, but Aaron hardly noticed.

He hadn't slept the night before. Images of Jesus kept flashing in his mind. He saw the lifeless body, the Roman spear, the long strips of linen. He remembered helping carry Jesus's cold form into the grim tomb and gently placing it down on the cold slab. He watched the soldiers strain as they pushed the massive stone over the opening, and he heard the loud thud as it sealed the Messiah into the grave.

Aaron had left the city while it slept. Now he stood on the Mount of Olives and looked back. The sun's rays touched the temple, and it glowed, yet to Aaron it was an insult. That building no longer symbolized the promised Messiah. It was the haunt of priests who paid thugs to condemn innocent men. It was a place that rejected him and threw him out. It was a sham.

Aaron sank to the ground. If the temple was corrupt and the Messiah was dead, then where should he turn? He buried his face into his hands and cried. He felt so alone and so sad.

"Aaron!" a voice cried out. "Aaron! Where are you?"

Aaron lifted his face and wiped away his tears. He saw an old man running up the trail. It was Nichodemus!

Aaron leaped to his feet and called out. Soon the old man was holding Aaron's hands as he tried to catch his breath. Nichodemus' face glowed with joy.

"I thought I might find you up here," the old priest said. "Your parents told me you left home while it was still dark." Nichodemus bent over and gulped air. "Whew, I'm too old to be running like this, but today I feel like a young man."

Aaron frowned. *What was wrong with Nichodemus?* he wondered.

Nichodemus straightened up and looked into Aaron's eyes. The old man's gaze sparkled as he spoke. "He's alive!"

Aaron didn't understand. "Who's alive?"

"Jesus!" Nichodemus grabbed Aaron's shoulders. "There was an emergency meeting of the Sanhedrin this morning. The soldiers guarding the tomb rushed in, and they looked terrified. They stammered about an earthquake and an angel. Then they all became quiet." Nichodemus swallowed hard. "Caiaphas ordered them to speak, and their commander described a Man, glowing like the sun, emerging from the tomb. He said the Man stood at the entrance and raised His hands in victory!"

"What?!" Aaron took a step back. "Do you mean that Jesus is alive?"

Nichodemus nodded vigorously. "Yes! The grave could not hold Him." Then the old man reverently spoke, "Everyone who believes in Him will have eternal life."

Aaron stood there dumbfounded. When the nation had rejected and killed Jesus, Aaron thought it was over, but now he saw the truth. The darkness can never defeat the light. He looked up at the bright morning sky and smiled.

Jesus was alive![45]

The Choice

Judgment Day is not about our righteousness or our sins. It's not about being good enough or forgiven or joining the right church. It's about looking into the face of Jesus and saying yes or no. It's about choosing the light or the darkness. It's a day of joy and love for those who say yes and follow Him. It's a day of sadness and despair for those who say no and walk away. Jesus believed each one of us was worth dying for. That was His judgment. Now He is holding out His hand to each of us. The ultimate decision is ours. Will we open the Christmas present? Will we come to the wedding feast? Will we let Him heal our blindness?

---

45   Matthew 27, 28

Main Points: I am fearless because …

God is good.

God judged me as worthy enough to die for.

God lets me judge Him.

God is with me.

Chapter 6

THE CHARACTER

"I have called you by name.
You are mine."[46]
— God

The Demons

An eerie scream pierced the cold night air. The hair on the back of Micah's neck stood straight up. He pulled his wet cloak tighter around his shoulders and rose to stoke the fire. *This is a spooky night*, Micah thought as he peered up at the night sky. The stars shone and the moon stood over the still lake.

Just an hour ago, things had been very different. An unexpected storm hit before the herdsmen could react. Fierce winds had screamed through their camp and knocked down their shelters. The thunder

---

46   Isaiah 43:1 NLT

had shaken the ground while lightning had rained down on the lake's surface and lit the night with its constant flashing. The rain had flown so hard it stung the men through their thin cloaks. Micah and his fellow herdsmen had huddled at the base of a giant rock shivering, drenched, and terrified.

Then the storm stopped. It didn't lose strength and turn to soft rain. It completely disappeared. One moment they were trying to survive in the middle of a gale, and the next all was silent stillness. The lightning, the wind, and the rain vanished as the last clap of thunder echoed from the hills across the lake. Unbelievably the storm was gone.

The men stared in shock at the calm waters and twinkling stars. A supernatural power had ended that violent storm, and they all felt it. Each man was soon lost in his own thoughts. Worry wrinkled each brow.

Micah shivered and built a fire. He was the youngest herder, so the fire was his responsibility. Soon the others gathered around the flames. No one spoke for a long time. Then one by one, each man left the fire and went to sleep until Micah was the last man awake.

Then the screams came from the graveyard on the other side of the ridge. The offshore breeze made the sounds seem closer than they actually were, but Micah did not feel safe. He had heard the stories.

Two men possessed by hundreds of demons roamed these hills. They slept in the tombs next to the bones of the dead. They ate raw animals they caught with their bare hands. Dirt and blood tangled their long strings of hair. Scars and cuts covered their filthy, naked bodies. Most people never saw them. But they could hear them.

The townspeople heard the screams on quiet nights. They heard unholy moans rise out of the stillness. They heard chains clinking in the darkness. The wild lunatics had been captured before. A squad of Roman soldiers on horseback had cornered both of them, thrown a net over them, and chained them to a tree. But in the middle of the night, the mad men had snapped their chains with superhuman strength and pounced on the soldiers, unleashing their fury. Soon the two monsters, with blood on their hands, fled into the black hills.

Now, no one dared to come anywhere near them. When people heard chains, they ran for their lives.

Micah's father had seen them once. He had been up in a tree harvesting fruit. The two crazy men had loped up the hill and stopped directly beneath his tree. His father had frozen, unmoving and unseen. From the safety of his perch, he had looked down on the men who grunted like pigs and smelled like death. They had stopped next to the ladder and sniffed the air. Terrified, Micah's father had prayed to the God of the Jews for protection. Then a noise had startled the two men, and they had bolted away.

"They are not men anymore," his father said. "They wear the mark of demons. They have become one with the darkness. Whoever they used to be is gone forever." Micah almost felt sorry for the demon-possessed men.

A shrill scream jolted Micah back into the present. He edged closer to the fire. Their wails and shrieks didn't sound angry. They sounded terrified. They sounded like they were being tortured.

Micah glanced over the lake and saw a group of boats coming to shore. The early morning light gave the boats the appearance of ghosts gliding across the still waters. They headed to a small beach at the foot of a large hill.

Micah turned back to the fire. It was dying. He got up, stretched, and grabbed some wood. Soon the fire grew into a nice blaze, and then he heard the screams again. This time they were closer, much closer.

Micah stood up quickly and grabbed his staff holding it like a weapon in front of him. Just then two men charged over the hill. Their wild hair flowed behind them. Their bodies were naked, and their eyes glowed. They came straight at the fire, straight toward him.

Micah screamed and ran. He didn't think about his friends. He didn't think about the pigs. He didn't think. He just ran. He ran for his life.

But the demon-crazed men did not chase Micah. They tore right through the middle of camp, crashing over sleeping men, tripping over the fire, knocking over pigs, leaving the camp in complete havoc, and then rushed toward the beach.

Breathing hard, Micah looked over his shoulder and quickly realized he was not in danger. He stopped running and bent over to catch his breath. His chest heaved, and his ears rang. He watched the lunatics race to the bottom of the hill.

Micah saw the unsuspecting sailors near their boats. At first, the boatmen didn't hear the demoniacs coming toward them, but suddenly the group splintered. Some men panicked, diving into the water. Others sprinted down the beach. A few climbed back into the boats and tried to hide. Everyone fled.

All except one. One Man bravely stood his ground unflinching. Micah squinted. This Man walked cooly toward the two possessed men. They were almost on Him. Micah feared this lone Man would be torn to shreds right before his eyes.

But the Man held up his hand, and the two demon-possessed men slammed to a stop, as if they had crashed into an invisible wall. They writhed and trembled.

Micah scrambled toward the beach. He wanted to see them. At this distance, he couldn't hear them, but he could tell that they were speaking. The men paced back and forth like caged animals, clawing their fingers at the other Man's face, but they came no closer. Micah peered at the lone Man standing courageously before such evil.

He was serene and still. Even from this distance, Micah sensed peace and power emanating out from Him. Micah began to jog toward the beach. Someone called for him to stop, but Micah ignored it. He had to see this Man up close. An unexplained desire pulled him to the Stranger on the shore.

Micah saw the Man raise His hand and point to the herd of pigs. Micah heard one strong word.

"Go!"

Both men dropped to the ground as if all the power had been sucked out of their bodies. A rush of ungodly wind howled right over Micah's head, and he threw himself to the sand as shrieks and screams whirled by. Micah curled into a ball petrified and waited for the demons to attack him. But in a flash, they were past him.

The demons hit the pigs without warning. One moment they were rooting around, lazy and calm, and the next moment the pigs screamed as if they were on fire. They reared and jumped and shook and shivered. Then controlled by one cruel mind, they charged to the edge of the steep hill and plummeted over the side. They tumbled and rolled and splashed into the dark water. Panicked, thrashing pigs fought and screeched on the surface for just a few moments. Then everything was quiet and still. The entire herd was gone.

Micah stared at the water. Then he looked back at the Man who was kneeling next to the two men on the ground. Micah got up and walked toward them. He wasn't sure what had happened. He heard the two men mumbling and saw the Man patting them on the back and speaking in a low, peaceful voice. The Man stood up and helped the two men to their feet, then called to His companions. Their eyes were wide, but they quickly brought some extra clothes. The whole group walked to the water's edge, and the two men scrubbed the filth off their bodies. Soon they were dressed and sitting at the feet of the Man who had freed them from the demons. Micah inched closer wanting to hear the conversation.

"Ask, and it will be given to you. Seek, and you will find," the Man smiled as He spoke. "Knock, and the door will be opened." The two sane men slowly nodded. "You no longer have to fear the demons," the Man continued. "You are sealed with my love. Call out to God when you are afraid or tempted, and He will give you the strength you need."

Micah forgot himself and soon stood right behind the two men. The Man noticed Micah and smiled at him. Micah looked down at the two men sitting in front of the Teacher. They were completely different. Their eyes were bright, and their voices were steady. One of them even laughed.

"How can we ever thank you?" one man asked. "You gave us our lives back."

"Don't thank Me," the Man pointed to the sky. "Thank your Father in Heaven. All good gifts come from Him." His eyes twinkled.

"Jesus," one of the men from the boat called out. "We've got a problem."

Micah looked and saw the other pig herders leading an angry mob toward the boats. Jesus walked out to meet the crowd. The lead herdsman fiercely pointed at Jesus, and the town elders stomped up to Him. They ranted and raved and shook their fists. Their eyes flashed with hate, and their bodies quaked with rage as they blamed Jesus for the missing herd of pigs. Then they demanded that He leave at once.

They look possessed, Micah thought.

Jesus nodded and walked back toward the group. "James," he said, "Get the boats ready. We're going back to the other side."

Micah's heart sank. *Jesus was leaving already?* The two restored men must have felt the same way, because they fell on their knees in front of Jesus and begged to go with Him.

One man promised, "I'll follow you wherever you go."

The Master smiled. "No," He said. "You have wives and children that need to see you. You have been gone far too long. Stay here and tell everyone the great things the Lord has done for you, and how He loves you and showed you mercy."

Jesus' followers were in the boats busy pulling ropes and breaking out the oars. Jesus touched each man on the shoulder and waded into the shallow water.

Micah stood on the beach. *What do I do?* he wondered. He wanted to go with Jesus.

Jesus was about to pull Himself into the boat, and then He stopped as if He remembered something. Jesus splashed back into the water and sloshed over to Micah. He was smiling. "You've had quite the morning, my friend," He said warmly.

Micah didn't know what to say. Jesus put both hands on Micah's shoulders and turned serious. "You saw something today that people in your town need to hear. Those two men over there, they will tell their story, but some will doubt because of their past. I am sending you to help them. Tell the people what you saw."

Jesus squeezed Micah's shoulders and winked. "You were made for more than herding pigs."

He started back to the boat.

Micah took one step after Him and found his voice, "Will I ever see you again?"

Jesus stopped and looked over His shoulder, "Yes. I will return." He smiled and jumped into a boat.

Micah watched the boats until they disappeared. He knew that his life would never be the same. There was something special about Jesus. His eyes, His smile, His words, they all had power, but not power like those demons. The power of the demons was scary. It hurt and controlled people. But Jesus' power was comforting. It helped people and set them free.

Micah wanted to see Jesus again. He started walking back to the town. It was time to tell his story.[47]

What Does God Want?

In this story, we see two men possessed by demons, marked by evil. Before Jesus healed them, they were lonely, hurting, naked, and miserable. Then Jesus freed them, clothed them, encouraged them, and believed in them. This story shows us a direct contrast between the character of evil and the character of God. It also shows us the human heart.

Everything flows out of the heart. Our words, our actions, our attitudes all come from the heart. At the end of time, there will be two types of people. One group will have the mark of the beast, and the other group will have the seal of God.

Jesus told a parable about the end of time. In His story, a king divided everyone into two groups. Jesus called them the sheep and the goats. This division was not arbitrary but based on the characters of each individual. The king praised the sheep for giving him food, water, and clothing. He thanked them for visiting him in prison and inviting him into their homes. But when the king turned his attention to the goats, he rebuked them for ignoring him when he was in need of food, water, and clothing. He asked them, "Why didn't you visit me in prison or invite me into your homes?"

---

47   Mark 5:1-20, Matthew 8:28-34

Both groups stammered in surprise, "Your majesty, we never saw you. We never helped you or ignored you." Then the king opened their eyes to reality.

He says, "Whatever you did for any of my subjects, you did to me."[48]

It is very important to notice that Jesus didn't mention a single religious act in this story but rather highlighted the difference of character traits between the sheep and the goats. He didn't talk about baptism, confession, communion, or even going to church. He talked about kindness.

Jesus shares the same principle again in the story of the Good Samaritan. The hero of the story was the man who helped a person in need, not the priest and Levite who kept all the right rules. Jesus wasn't throwing out all the religious traditions of the Jews. He explained that those rules, traditions, feast days, and ceremonies pointed to a God of love. They were teaching tools designed to help humanity connect to the heart of God. This connection would transform them, heal them, save them. The tragedy Jesus warned about was keeping every tradition and obeying every commandment and yet missing out on God's love. It would be like sitting down at Thanksgiving dinner and only looking at the food. It doesn't matter how perfect people's table manners are, if they don't eat, then they are still hungry.

---

48   Matthew 25:31-46

Jesus came to set the Jews straight and shift their focus from their actions to their hearts. He told people that what they eat doesn't make them unclean, but what comes from the heart is what makes them dirty.[49] His showed us that the commandments on murder and adultery started in the heart long before they became sinful behaviors.[50] Jesus tried to wake the Pharisees up by calling them whitewashed tombs.[51] He knew that even though on the outside they kept the rules and looked perfect, on the inside they were full of hate and death. They needed new hearts. That's all Jesus wants. He wants the heart. He wants to fill it with His love and joy and peace. Then the behavior will change. But He starts on the inside.

The Seal of God

"... we have placed the seal of God
on the foreheads of His servants."
— Revelation 7:3

The seal of God rests on the foreheads of God's people. These individuals are represented by the sheep in the previous parable. The seal symbolizes a changed mindset, a Christlike character, a new heart. When a believer accepts the Holy Spirit

---

49   Matthew 15:11

50   Matthew 5:17-30

51   Matthew 23:27-28

into their hearts, they are sealed,[52] and the fruits of the Holy Spirit flow out of the believer's heart.[53] Being sealed is not a physical mark but a character transformation.

Striving to maintain Christian standards of behavior before being filled by the Holy Spirit leads to frustration and failure. Paul warned the Romans. "Don't conform to the pattern of this world, but be transformed by the renewing of your mind."[54] Conformity cares about outward appearances. It is all about fitting in. But to be transformed means that a change starts on the inside.[55] The Greek word for *renew* can also mean *renovate*. Paul invited his readers to let God renovate their hearts and minds.

The forehead protects the prefrontal cortex, the place in the brain where a person feels empathy and love, where people decide between right and wrong, where people experience spirituality. The seal on the forehead symbolizes a Christlike mindset. Jesus comes in and renovates a person by replacing selfishness and fear with His love and faith. The focus shifts from self to God. The character becomes noble; the heart becomes pure. This new mindset transforms the outward behavior, and the sheep keep the commandments of God and are faithful to Jesus.[56]

---

52   Ephesians 1:12

53   Galatians 5:22—love, joy, peace, patience, kindness, goodness, faithfulness, gentleness, self control

54   Romans 12:2

55   https://biblehub.com/greek/342.htm

56   Revelation 14:12

The act of worship, the focused attention on God's character, naturally changes the human mind. As we see the Lamb of God, we become like Him. We see how He loved everyone, and our hearts become more and more like Jesus. We may still observe the rituals of our church, but instead of empty habits, these rituals become fresh and full of meaning. We see Jesus in the symbols of our church services, which bring tears to our eyes and joy to our souls. We come alive with light and peace. Then we may work in a mission field or lead a small Bible study. We may have our whole lives turned upside down, or our circumstances may stay the same. But lives will be different because our hearts are different.

The test will come. Everyone must walk through the valley of fire. Like a kiln turns clay into pottery, flames solidify our choices and cement our hearts. Sometimes this process happens individually, but before the end of time, there will be a worldwide test of loyalty. It may center around an outward religious ceremony, but the conflict is for the heart. Like Jesus in the Garden of Gethsemane, everyone will decide to trust in God or trust in self. We will choose between love and selfishness.

This test of character happens daily on a smaller scale, but the trial by fire is coming. The best way to prepare for the moment of conflict is to focus on Jesus, to see Him, to fall in love with Him. This is true worship. Then nothing can drag us away, nothing can convince us to cheat on Him, nothing can make us turn our backs on Him. To focus on Jesus is a daily decision, and in time, the results show up in a person's character. Like the disciples, people will say, "They have been with Jesus."[57] This is the destiny of all the sheep.

The Mark of the Beast

"Anyone who worships the beast and
his statue or who accepts his mark
on the forehead or on the hand..."
—Revelation 14:9

The mark of the beast sits on the forehead or the hand of those who reject God. They are the goats and have very different characters than the sheep. The mark of the beast is not a tattoo, a microchip, a vaccine, or any other physical object. It is the character of a lost soul.

The character of the beast is very different from the Lamb's. It is a dangerous animal with powerful claws and sharp fangs. The beast conquers and kills to get what it wants, while the Lamb of God gently walks to the cross to die for us. The noble, self-sacrificing lamb stands next to the bloodthirsty, violent beast. Jesus leads by example and gives us the freedom to choose for ourselves, while the beast rules through dominating force and seeks to control us.

---

57   Acts 4:13

In the book of Daniel, there are many visions with beasts, and they all represented kingdoms that ruled through dominance, force, and fear. The beasts in Revelation 13 resemble many of the animals from Daniel's visions. These beasts speak arrogantly and blaspheme God. They war against the saints and force the world to worship their way. They use economic sanctions, threats, persecutions, and murder to force humanity to conform to their theology. Everyone who submits to the leadership of the beast takes its mark and becomes like it.

Revelation 14:9 says that people *lambano* the mark of the beast. Many translations interpret this word as *to receive*, which places people's destiny in someone else's hands. Who is giving people the mark of the beast? Is it God, Satan, or a world leader? People worry about being good enough, joining the right church, and following the right rules. They don't want to make a mistake and receive the mark of the beast. But a more accurate translation is *to take or accept. Lambano* literally means *to take with the hand.*[58] It means to pick something up and hold it. A better translation says that people accept or pick up the mark of the beast. The mark of the beast is not given; it is taken. This understanding of *lambano* gives us the responsibility. No one holds our eternity in their hands. We have the choice to take the mark of the beast or to push it away.

---

58   https://biblehub.com/greek/2983.htm

The mark of the beast shows up in two places, the forehead and the hand.[59] Remember, the forehead protects the part of the brain where we choose between right and wrong. The mark on the forehead represents a chosen mindset, and those with the mindset of the beast reject God's love and instead grab selfishness. This choice dries up all feelings of empathy and kindness. Instead of becoming one with God, the person who takes the mark on their forehead becomes intimate with evil. They are like the demon-possessed men. They become tools of the devil and degenerate into selfishness and cruelty, which naturally results in their pain and suffering. Their minds are marked with hate.

The mark on the hand symbolizes a group of people who align with the beast through their actions but who don't necessarily believe. They feel the pressure to conform, and they get in line even though they believe the action is wrong. This group is conflicted because they know in their hearts the right choice, but they fail to trust God. They reject the seal of God and take the easy path. Their hearts are not fully given to the darkness, but they act like the beast. Satan and his followers don't care if a person takes the mark on their forehead or their hand. They don't care if people truly believe or just go along with the crowd. They only want outward compliance and total control.

---

59   Revelation 14:9

The followers of the beast take his character. They lose their nobility and descend into selfishness. They become willing to sacrifice others for their safety and security. These people become comfortable with the tactics of coercion, threats, and even violence. They become controlling and dominate just like their leader. The mark of the beast on their foreheads or hands seeps into their character.

The difference is simple. The Lamb wants a relationship and is willing to die to earn that love, while the beast wants submission and is willing to kill to gain that power over people. The final conflict of the world is between these two leaders. Everyone will pick a side, and everyone's character will reflect that decision.

The Trap

If mainstream Christianity claims that God is a Dominance leader, that His law is imposed, that He uses force to control us, that He demands obedience and good works for salvation, then the god they take to the world is actually the beast. They put wolf's clothing on the Lamb of God and spread a message of fear while calling it the Gospel. This distorted teaching contradicts the life, teachings, and death of Jesus and sets up the world to accept the mark of the beast. The world believes the lie that God behaves like the beast.

The Gospel truth is that God is an Influence leader, that His law is natural, that He gives us the freedom to choose, that He wants our worship and our hearts, that He has already judged us and waits for us to judge Him. This is the Father that Jesus showed us. This is the God who gave His only Son to die for us. This is love, and we know it. This truth brings peace and transforms us from scared sinners into courageous Christ-followers. This truth must be shared.

Our Choice

We all will choose between these two gods. Just as those who follow the Lamb become more like Jesus, those who take the mark of the beast become more like Satan. They are fearful and use fear to manipulate others. They use force in the name of good. This is the spirit of the Inquisition, of the Crusades, of all the persecutions that imprisoned, tortured, stoned, and burned good men and women in all ages. People with the mark of the beast are like the Pharisees. They look religious and perfect on the outside, but they will do anything to gain control.

At the end of time, there will be only sheep and goats. One group will try to eliminate the other with force, while the other leaves people free to decide for themselves. One will be filled with hate, and the other will be filled with love. One will have torment, and the other will have peace. One will gnash their teeth, while the other will praise God. This difference is not a curse from God, but the natural result of worship. One group mutates into a shadow of the beast, while the other reflects the loving character of the Lamb. One group will resemble the demon-possessed men. They may not run around screaming and cutting themselves, but their hearts will be full of terror and hate and darkness. They have taken the mark of the beast. The other group will resemble these very same men after Jesus rescued them. They will be calm, in control, and sitting at the feet of Jesus, ready to follow Him in the boats or to go back home and tell His story. God has sealed their hearts with His love, and it shows.

Meant for More

The next day Micah saw the two healed men in the marketplace and stopped to listen. Both men were dressed nicely and had trimmed hair and beards. They looked strong and noble, so different than before they met Jesus. One stood on a cart and began to tell his story. The man talked about how a little, hidden sin grew and grew until he was no longer in control of his mind. He spoke of terror and pain. His words were magnetic. Soon another person stopped to listen, then another. In a few minutes, a small crowd had gathered around.

Then the man spoke of Jesus. He told how even in the thick cloud of darkness, he felt the light. He spoke of yearning to be free and the Man on the beach. He said that when he opened his mouth to beg for help, the demons spoke instead. Then Jesus commanded the demons to leave.

The man paused and with tears in his eyes said, "When the demons released me, I could breathe again. I could see again. The world became so bright. Then Jesus knelt beside me. He touched me, and I ..." his voice cracked. He was silent for several long moments. "I looked into His eyes. Jesus loved me. There I was dirty, bloody, naked, and ashamed, but He loved me." The man bowed his head overcome with emotion.

The other man put his hand on his friend's shoulder and continued, "This Teacher's name is Jesus of Nazareth. He spoke, and the demons fled. He touched us, and we were healed. The Lord has done this great thing for us. He showed us mercy. Somehow, He heard our cries for help beneath the stranglehold of the demons. I know that the Lord can do great things for you too. If He can show me mercy, then surely He will help you."

Then one of them pointed straight at Micah. "You were there yesterday," he said. "I remember you."

Micah gulped and nodded as everyone's eyes turned to him. Micah remembered the Master's words. "Tell the people what you saw." His palms were sweaty, and his mouth was dry. Micah looked at the crowd and was terrified.

Before he could change his mind, Micah took a deep breath, stepped forward, and shared his story. "I was sound asleep when the storm hit. The thunder and lightning was so intense I could barely breathe, but then the storm stopped in one moment." Micah nodded at the two men. "That's when I first heard their screams."

Micah continued to tell his story, and the words flowed. He described the early morning fire and how terrifying it was as the two demoniacs bolted through the camp. The people gasped when he described the two madmen tumbling over the sleeping herdsmen. He talked about the lone Man on the beach.

"Jesus didn't run away like everyone else. He is too brave. He held up His hand, and those two dropped to the ground." Micah laughed nervously. "Jesus told the demons to go, and they obeyed."

Micah closed his eyes as he walked through the memories. He felt the rush of wind, heard the screams of the pigs, and saw Jesus' face. He couldn't help but smile. Micah described the chaos of the pigs rushing into the lake and the strange silence afterwards.

"What is Jesus like?" a woman holding a basket asked.

Micah tried to capture the experience with words. "He's good. I could feel it, but at the same time, He's so powerful. Those demons were terrified of Him, but somehow I wasn't." Micah stopped and thought about Jesus.

"Jesus made me feel special. He had just performed a huge miracle, and yet He took the time to speak to me. He told me I was meant for more than herding pigs." Micah took a deep breath. "Jesus is going to come back. He wants to help more people, but we have to let Him stay. We can't send Him away again."

Micah walked over and stood between the two men. "Look at these guys. Look at what Jesus did. Before He came, they were scary and dangerous, but after meeting Jesus, they changed."

When Micah finished, everything was silent. Then a man asked the question that was on everyone's mind.

"Is Jesus the Messiah?"

Everyone looked at the three storytellers expectantly. The two men glanced at each other and nodded, but Micah was the one who spoke.

"They say He calmed the storm. We saw Him defeat the demons. Who else could He be?"

That answer was good enough for the crowd, and slowly they dispersed. Some were lost in thought, while others talked in small groups.

Micah grinned and felt so alive. He was a servant of the Messiah, and just now he had felt the bravery of Jesus. At first he had been petrified, but after he started talking, a peace flooded into his heart. Micah wanted to laugh out loud.

Soon only three men stood in the square. The two men looked directly at Micah and smiled. One of them waved his hand and said, "Come, my friend. We are going to the next town. Join us."

Micah turned to the two men and nodded his head. *I was made for this,* he thought. He pictured Jesus' face and heard Him say, "Tell the people what you saw." He knew that this was his moment. It was time to step into the unknown.

Micah took a deep breath and made his decision. "Yes. I'll go with you." He smiled as a warm sense of peace filled his heart. He had made the right choice.

That had been the beginning. The trio had talked in every town in the region to anyone who would listen. They couldn't answer all the questions and didn't know the prophecies about the Messiah, but they could tell their story. So they did again and again and again.

The Return

Then one day Jesus returned.

"He's back!" someone shouted. Feet rushed down the street. Micah leaned out of the doorway and saw a friend.

"What's all the fuss about?" he asked.

His friend barely stopped. "Jesus, the one with the demons and the pigs. He's at the beach!" Then his friend was gone.

Micah grabbed his cloak off the bench and ran outside to join the crowd rushing to the beach. Jesus stood on the hill near the spot where Micah had built a little fire. It seemed that the entire town surrounded him. Micah saw more people coming from other towns.

Jesus was telling a story to a group of children sitting at His feet, but His voice carried all the way to the back of the group. Micah edged his way through the crowd, and when he got to the front, he saw Jesus and smiled. His heart felt warm.

"Then the Master will return …" Jesus stopped in the middle of a sentence. He reached out a hand and motioned for Micah to stand next to Him. Embarrassed and awkward, Micah stepped forward and came to Jesus. He glanced up and saw that everyone was looking at him.

Micah gulped, but felt better when Jesus put His arm around the young man's shoulders and warmly continued. "Then the Master will return and say, 'Well done, my good and faithful servant.'" He squeezed Micah's shoulders and looked out over the growing crowd. "Well done," Jesus said quietly. "Well done."

The Results of Our Choice

The mark of the beast and the seal of God are two paths. Each path is sculpted in the image of its leader. God stands on one side for truth, love, and freedom, while on the other side Satan crouches with lies, selfishness, and control. This evil angel is the mastermind behind every false god. Satan's greatest deception is to paint his character traits on God. This false god shares the same name and claims the same power as the true God, but beneath the veneer of holiness, its character reeks of force and violence. This god is a dictator who demands obedience and wields his divine power to coerce and control. The true God is the Creator who built the Universe, understands its laws, and teaches us how to live in harmony with them. While both powers promise eternal life for believers who trust in them, only God earns that trust by dying to prove it. The other god demands outward compliance.

The battle between good and evil is fought in our hearts and minds. Two very different views of God struggle for our loyalty. Everyone has a choice, and that choice will determine if we live our lives fully now as well as shape our eternal destiny. All of us will declare for one of the two gods. That decision will echo in our characters and will slowly transform our hearts into the very image of the god we choose. That is why it is vital for the Gospel, the good news of God's loving character, to go out. Many believe pagan fables packaged in Christian wrapping paper. They serve the right name but the wrong character. Their fear of the god they worship is evidence that they doubt their god's goodness and unconditional love. True love casts out fear.[60] When the real nature of God is understood, Christians will

---

60   1 John 4:18

not be afraid. They will be bold as lions and soar on wings of eagles.[61]

It is time to learn the truth. The day of confusion is over. Clarity has arrived. Now we stand in the valley of decision, and our eternity hangs in the balance. The true God leads us to freedom and joy, while Satan drags us into captivity and despair.

The Lord

"The Lord is the son of El," the high priest paused and looked over the quiet room of boys. "He gives us rain and makes our crop grow. He guides the sun on its path across the sky with wisdom and power."

Everyone's eyes were wide as the priest taught. It was a great honor to have the high priest come and teach a lesson. Each boy in the room dreamed of one day joining the ranks of the priesthood and standing at the altar.

The high priest patted one boy on the head. "And what must we do to earn this favor?" he asked.

The boy did not hesitate. "We must obey the Lord and serve Him with our whole hearts."

The old man smiled, "Good answer." Then he walked to another boy and looked him in the eye. "And why do we love the Lord?"

The little boy gulped and turned bright red. He stammered and mumbled and then hung his head in shame. The high priest saw an opportunity.

---

61   Proverbs 28:1, Isaiah 40:31

"What is your name, son?" the priest asked.

The little boy swallowed hard. "My name is Ammiel, sir."

"Come here, Ammiel," the priest commanded. The boy was fighting back tears, but he bravely stood in front of the class. The high priest put a hand on the Ammiel's thin shoulders.

"Who can tell us about the prophecy?" he questioned.

Dozens of hands shot up in the air. The priest pointed to a large boy with freckles. "You. Stand up and tell us what you know."

The boy shot up out of his seat and began to speak. His voice cracked, and snickers rippled through the room. The priest frowned, and the laughter vanished. The boy with the freckles took a deep breath and tried again.

"The prophecy says that the Lord will fight the great serpent Leviathan and the god of death and that he-"

"And what is the god of death's name?" the priest interrupted.

The boy's eyes got wide and the color drained from his face. Someone whispered near him, and he stuttered, "M-m-mot. Sir, the god's name is Mot."

"And what happens in that great battle between the good and evil?" the priest asked and then patted the little boy's shoulder who stood next to him. "My young friend, Ammiel, wants to know."

The boy with the freckles nodded and continued. "In the battle, the serpent and Mot kill the Lord, but the Lord comes back to life."

"Very good," the priest said. "You may sit down."

The boy with the freckles breathed a sigh of relief and plopped down.

The priest turned to Ammiel and began to teach. "The Lord defeated death, and He will bestow the gift of eternal life to those who please Him. That is our job as priests. We must teach the people how to win the Lord's favor."

Ammiel fidgeted. The priest continued, "Do you want to help people when you grow up?"

The boy nodded.

"Then you must study hard and learn everything you can, for the Lord is loving and full of blessings, but remember that the Lord is also just. He knows that we are evil and full of sin, and He knows that when we offer the proper sacrifice we experience a little bit of His death. This pleases Him and opens the gates for His blessings to rain down on us," the priest lectured.

Ammiel stopped nodding and frowned. The priest noticed the change and tilted his head.

"Do you have a question, my son?" the old man asked.

Ammiel was thinking. He was no longer self conscious. He looked up at the priest. "If the Lord is the god of the rain, and if we are giving him all the right sacrifices, then why hasn't it rained in years?"

The priest's expression darkened. The boy was right. It had nearly been three years since the last rainfall. The fields were parched, and the animals were dying. The country was on the verge of ruin.

The priest took a deep breath. "The Lord holds back the rain because we have not yet done enough to earn His blessings. He expects obedience and faithfulness, and our nation continues to earn His wrath by clinging to the old ways. He is testing our faith and our willingness to sacrifice."

The priest stepped closer to Ammiel and loomed over him. "I wonder if you would be willing to make the ultimate sacrifice for the Lord." The priest's eyes flashed with evil.

Ammiel froze in terror. He had never seen a child sacrifice, but he had heard the stories.

Just then the door burst open and another priest rushed into the room.

"He's back! Elijah is back!"

The high priest whipped around in horror. "What did you say!?"

The other priest bent over, out of breath. He forced himself to speak through gasps for air. "Elijah showed up out of nowhere. He met the king. Then he ordered everyone in Israel to gather at Mt. Carmel." The priest wiped the sweat from his brow. "He called for all the priests of our Lord Baal and the sacred goddess Asherah to be present as well."

The high priest smiled wickedly. "So the troublemaker has trapped himself." He folded his arms across his chest. "He will be outnumbered, and Baal, the Lord, will have his victory."[62]

The two men hurried out of the room, and chaos erupted as the boys talked excitedly about the gathering. Only one person stood quietly, the little boy at the front of the room.

Ammiel was shaking with fear. The priest had threatened to use him as the next child sacrifice, and he was terrified. He had tried to be good, but he had forgotten the answer when the priest had called on him. Did this mean that he wasn't good enough? Ammiel's stomach hurt.

His uncle worshipped the God of Elijah and called Him the Lord. Baal was also called the Lord, but the two gods seemed very different to the little boy. Baal frightened him with his endless rules and threats, but his uncle's God seemed safer and somehow comforting. Ammiel remembered the stories his uncle told around the fire at night. His favorite was the story about the shepherd who fought a giant with the Lord's help.

---

62   Wood, D. R. W., and Marshall, I. H. *New Bible Dictionary*, 3rd ed. (1996), 108.).

Miller, Patrick.*Israelite Religion and Biblical Theology: Collected Essays.* (Continuum International Publishing Group, 2000), 32.

Moscati, Sabatino. *The Phoenicians*, (Tauris, 2001), 132.
Walbank, Frank William. *A Historical Commentary on Polybius*, Volume 2. (Clarendon Press, 1979), 47.

Zondervan's Pictorial Bible Dictionary, 1976.

By then, the room had emptied as the boys rushed home to tell their parents about the gathering on Mt. Carmel. Ammiel blinked; he was confused. There were two gods with the same name, who did the same things, who claimed the same devotion. Which one should he serve? Which one was the true god?

Ammiel turned to leave and hoped that by the end of the day he would know the answer.

Mt. Carmel

The little boy's sweaty hand held tightly to his uncle's. He was hot and thirsty. His uncle, Malachi, bent down and offered him the last sip from the skin of water.

"That's the last of it," Malachi said as he playfully ruffled the boy's hair. Then he stood and looked at the mob of priests dancing and chanting around the altar to Baal. He snorted, "Those fools have been at it all day long." He took the empty skin from the little boy's hand and lifted him up on his shoulders. "Ammiel, take a look for yourself."

Ammiel squinted in the late afternoon sunlight and shielded his eyes with his hand. The priests had set up a perimeter so no one could come close to Baal's sacred altar. Ammiel spotted the high priest who had been in his classroom earlier. The man was holding a golden dagger and covered in his own blood.

Ammiel heard the high priest crying out in anguish. "Oh Lord of heaven and earth, send us the holy fire from your throne and prove to all that you are the true god!" He lifted his arm and pulled down his sleeve. "See my devotion!" he shrieked as he made a long cut down his arm. Ammiel closed his eyes in horror, but soon opened them to see what would happen next.

Blood flowed down the high priest's arm and onto his rich tunic. The drums beat louder, and the other priests began another dance. Ammiel's heart thudded loudly, but nothing happened. There was no fire. There was no answer.

Then a man stood and walked toward the staggering high priest. This man wore a short leather tunic and had wild hair. The other priest stumbled out of his way as he walked with firm, confident steps.

"That's Elijah, the prophet of the Lord," Malachi whispered.

Elijah stood in front of the high priest. The contrast between the two men was so powerful that even Ammiel could feel it. Elijah looked regal and peaceful even as his hair blew in the breeze. Baal's high priest looked exhausted and defeated in his blood soaked clothes. The men glared at each other, and the crowd waited breathlessly to see what would happen.

The high priest couldn't hold the prophet's steady gaze, and the wounded man turned away and staggered into the arms of another priest before he fainted to the ground weak from loss of blood.

Elijah spoke to the people in a clear, calm voice. "Come closer." He motioned for the people to approach and began to build an altar. As he worked, the people slowly came closer.

Malachi's strong hands held Ammiel steady on his shoulders as he moved forward. "Do you see the two altars?" he asked his nephew.

Ammiel nodded, too thirsty to speak.

Malachi continued, "The altar of Baal is made from stone cut in far away quarries. See how smooth the edges are, how perfect the stones fit together?"

The crowd pressed in around Elijah. The prophet's arms bulged as he hefted large stones into place. "Now look at the prophet's altar, uncut stones, taken from the ground of this mountain." Malachi paused. "Those stones represent the worshippers of each god. Baal demands perfection, but God will use anyone who is willing, even common stones with rough edges. See. The prophet is choosing twelve stones, one for each of the tribes of Israel."

Ammiel thought about his uncle's words. His God seemed so different from the god he learned about in class.

Elijah finished building the altar. He turned to a nearby servant and ordered him to get the water. Ammiel didn't understand.

"Don't worry, little nephew," Malachi sensed the boy's unease. "The prophet knows what he is doing. Remember what he said at the beginning of the day?"

Ammiel thought back to the morning. It seemed like so long ago. "He said, 'If the Lord is God, follow Him, but if Baal is god, then follow him.'"

"Our nation has wavered between two gods for long enough. It's time to choose. It's time to stand up for the true Lord." Malachi's grip tightened on Ammiel's ankles. "I will stand with Elijah," he said quietly. "I'm done hiding."

Soon the servant came and dumped water all over the altar. "Now no one can claim that Elijah used trickery to light the fire," Malachi explained. He looked at the sun and said, "It's time for the evening sacrifice."

Elijah ordered the servant to douse the altar again. Then again. The people murmured at the waste of so much water during the drought, but no one dared to stop Elijah. The prophet moved with holy strength and carried an aura of sacredness that kept the crowd silent and respectful.

Ammiel looked at the altar. The offering was drenched with water filling up a ditch Elijah had dug. The prophet walked around the altar and then raised his hands toward heaven.

"O Lord, God of Abraham, Issac, and Israel, today let it be known that You are God," the prophet's confident words rang out over the crowd. Elijah's voice was calm, as if he was talking to a friend. "Answer me, O Lord, so that your people may know you."

The prophet's words hung in the dry air, when a crack of thunder rocked the mountain. Ammiel instinctively ducked, and his uncle jerked downward in fright. A loud roar shook the very ground, and Ammiel looked up. A hole had opened in the sky, and a giant streak of white light tore straight for the mountaintop. Fire blasted into the altar in a blinding flash and terrific crash. The ground shook as the fire poured onto the altar, and Ammiel's mouth dropped open as he watched the offering, the stones, and even the water in the ditch disappear in the white fire.

Malachi pulled Ammiel down off of his shoulders and bowed his head to the ground. "The Lord," he said reverently, "The Lord, He is God."

Ammiel bowed to the ground too. His heart pounded, but it wasn't from fear. He was excited, for now he knew which lord was the true God. In that moment, the boy vowed to serve the Lord for the rest of his days.[63]

The Power Is in Our Hands

Every person holds their eternal destiny in their hands. Instead of reacting to this responsibility with fear, we must see it as a gift. Evil can threaten us, but it cannot control us unless we let it. No one needs to

---

63   1 Kings 18:16-45

be afraid of the mark of the beast. It is a character that is selfish, fearful, and willing to hurt others.

The seal of God is when the Holy Spirit comes into our hearts and begins to transform us into the likeness of God. We may not be perfect, but we will experience the fruits of the Spirit. We will love people and be willing to sacrifice for the good of others.

We have the power to choose. Now we know the truth. We can see the two choices, and we know the results of both choices. Will we fall at the feet of Jesus or send Him away? Will we stand with Elijah or the priests of Baal?

Main Points: I am fearless because ...
God is good.
God will not give me the Mark of the Beast. It is something I choose.
God will seal me with His character as I choose love and kindness.
God is with me.

Chapter 7

THE INVITATION

"Come to me if you are tired
and carry heavy burdens.
I will give you rest."[64]
—Jesus

The Call

His arms were on fire. He pulled and strained on
the cold, soggy nets. Sweat dripped into his eyes.
He blinked hard, but did not wipe away the sting.
Instead he kept tugging. His nets were heavy but
not heavy enough. His weathered fingers could feel
the slight twitch or hard jerk if the catch was good,
but tonight no life struggled as he pulled them up
from the black depths. With an exhausted grunt, he
heaved the rest of the water logged nets back into

---

64   Based on multiple translations of Matthew 11:28

his old boat. Empty! They were completely, utterly empty. There wasn't even a single, stinking minnow.

Simon let loose a string of curse words. His brother Andrew didn't even look up, he too felt like cursing. For weeks, the brothers had worked like slaves all night long, but their measly catches could barely feed their hungry families. There was nothing extra for the market. Food supplies were running low. Their wives looked anxious.

Being a fisherman was hard. The long nights were exhausting. The hard work was dangerous. The cold sea was unforgiving. But Simon felt that the fickle fish were the worst part. Sometimes the fish came and the nets were heavy. But recently even the most seasoned fishermen were returning empty handed.

Some chalked it up to the unusually hot weather, which drove the fish into deeper water far past the reach of the nets. Others said it was a curse from God for the sins of the Jewish nation. Simon couldn't care less about theories or theology. He just wanted to catch fish. No. He needed to catch fish! He desperately needed to catch fish. Simon spat in frustration, stood, and threw his nets out again. And again. And again.

But all night long the nets came up empty. Early dawn rose to full sun, and Simon knew that fishing now was useless. The fish in Lake Galilee had keen eyesight, and the crystal waters ensured that they never swam into the nets during the day. Any more tosses would only be a waste of effort. Simon cursed again and angrily gave the signal, and the fishermen quit for the day.

As he rowed hard, Simon thought about his life. With each thrust of the oars, the accusing voice in his head got louder. He tried to ignore it. Counter it. Argue against it. But after this exhausting night he didn't have the strength to fight anymore. He just needed to accept the plain truth in his head. No matter how hard he tried, he was never good enough. Like this night of fishing, his life was a disappointment. He thought about his marriage, his reputation, his character, and his future. He sighed and shook his head. He worked hard, but he always came up short. Looking at the soggy pile of empty nets, he thought, *I'm not even a good fisherman.*

Simon's shoulders slumped, *God must be so disappointed in me!*

The bow scraped against the rocky beach. He sighed then slowly stood up and began to clamor over the side of his boat.

"Fisherman," a deep strong voice rang out.

Simon stopped and looked up. A Man walked toward him then stood at the edge of the water. He smiled.

"May I use your boat?" he asked.

Simon rolled his eyes. "Do I look like a tour guide?" he almost retorted.

But the Man interrupted his thoughts motioning to the crowd sitting on the shore. "I am teaching these people, and there's no more room on the beach. If I could stand in your boat and push out just a bit, then everyone could see and hear what I have to say."

The Man smiled again as he waited for Simon's answer.

Simon huffed. He was tired, and his back ached. But there was something intriguing about this Teacher. Simon normally didn't like the teachers of the law. They were arrogant and haughty with clean fingernails and smooth uncalloused hands, too pure to get dirty with real men's work. But this Teacher seemed different. Simon shrugged. What did it matter? He could mend nets in the boat while the Teacher talked. He held out his hand.

The Teacher nodded His thanks, strode into the water, and grabbed Simon's hand. Surprisingly, the Teacher's hand was coarse and strong. Simon pulled Him up into the boat. Their eyes met, and the fisherman felt the Teacher read into his empty, pathetic soul. Embarrassed, Simon quickly looked away. The Teacher smiled kindly at Simon before He began a story. His deep voice rippled over the water.

"The Kingdom of Heaven is like a rich man who sent out invitations for his wedding."

Simon plopped down in the stern and methodically worked through his nets, checking for rips, frayed edges, and whatever could weigh them down tonight. Soon Simon was listening intently to the Teacher's story, and the next, and the next. *No one speaks like this man*, he thought. After what seemed a few minutes, the Teacher looked at the sun. It was high and hot.

"Well, friends, that is all today. Now, please excuse me," the Teacher grinned mischievously. "I'm going fishing." The people on the shore laughed at the joke.

Simon pushed the nets off his lap and started to get up. "Fisherman," the Teacher said, "Push your boat into deeper water and throw your nets out."

Simon shot a quick look at Andrew. This Teacher was a great storyteller, but he obviously didn't know about fish.

"Teacher," Simon began patiently, "We've been fishing all night. We didn't catch a single fish. There's no way we're catching anything in broad daylight. It's impossible."

The Teacher smiled. "With God all things are possible."

Simon started to argue, but Andrew put a calm hand on his shoulder. "Ok!" Simon threw his hands up in the air. "You win."

Simon pushed the boat out and picked up the nets.

"Give it a good throw," the Teacher said.

Simon nodded and just for show heaved the heavy nets out as far as he could. They splashed in the sparkling water and quickly sank from view. Simon wondered just how long he should entertain the naive Teacher before hauling in the empty nets.

Suddenly the nets surged downward as if a giant hand from the depths had reached up and grabbed them. The boat lurched forward, and

Simon momentarily lost his balance. He grabbed a fistfull of the netting and started to pull, but it was wrenched from his hands. Simon clenched his teeth and called for Andrew's help.

The next few minutes were chaotic. Initially, Simon's boat was jerked hard in the direction of the nets and began to glide across the water. Simon laughed. There were so many fish, they pulled the boat. Then in a panic the fish dove. The boat tipped precariously to the side and took on water. Frantically Simon and Andrew yelled for help. James and John's boat appeared alongside, and soon both boats were sinking.

Muscles strained, and men grunted. Simon glanced over to see the Teacher grabbing the nets, pulling and working right alongside Andrew. The Teacher's tunic was soaked, His hair wet, His smile huge. With almost superhuman strength, the men coaxed the surging nets upward.

When they finally made it to the surface, the fish went mad, churning the blue water white. The fishermen whooped with joy, slapped each other on the back, and rowed slowly back to shore. The pair of boats were so low in the water every wave splashed into the hold.

Simon had never seen so many fish in one place, and he was a fisherman! This was the biggest catch of his entire life. He could pay his bills, refit his ship, and buy his wife that bracelet she had wanted for years. Simon laughed with joy like a little boy. He forgot about his aching back and tired arms.

The two boats finally reached the shore, and the fishermen dragged the nets onto the beach. Simon looked again at the Teacher. His eyes twinkled, and He motioned for Simon to come closer. Exhausted but elated, Simon staggered over to Him. He was a simple fisherman, and not a very good one at that, but for some amazing reason, he was in the presence of more than a good Teacher. Surely this Man was the long-awaited Messiah. He felt painfully ashamed of his selfishness, his coarseness, and his complaining. He felt too dirty to be this close to Someone so good. He fell to his knees.

"Leave me alone," Simon said, his eyes filling with tears of shame. "I'm not good enough." But even as the words left his mouth, Simon wanted nothing more than to be in this Teacher's presence forever.

"Simon," the Teacher's voice was strong and happy. "Look at me."

Slowly Simon looked up into a face filled with love and acceptance. He forgot about the fish and his fears as his eyes met the Teacher's. This was it! This was what he'd been looking for. For the first time in his life, Simon felt content and completely safe. He couldn't help but smile.

Then the Teacher spoke, "Follow me."

Simon's heart lurched. This was the call of a rabbi! Fishermen were never called to be followers, yet here was a Teacher calling him to become a disciple.

"Teacher," Simon said, "I'm just a fisherman."

"Oh, I see much more than a fisherman," the Teacher chuckled.

Simon looked again, this time directly into the Teacher's eyes. Then he spoke from the depths of his heart, "Yes, Jesus! Yes! I will follow you anywhere!"

Jesus smiled and pulled Simon to his feet. He slung His arm over Simon's shoulders and said, "Come with me, and I'll teach you how to fish for men." Then He winked, and together they walked back to the nets.

"We've got a lot of work to do," Simon said as he bent over and sorted the fish.

The Teacher looked out over the lake and to its surrounding hills. "Yes, we do, Simon. Yes, we do."[65]

Today

The world today is full of confusion and darkness. Pandemics, riots, natural disasters, and political instability fill the news while personal tragedies, disease, financial stress, and heartbreak claw at our hearts. There has never been a time in world history when the truth has been so desperately needed. Many Christian denominations take a weak gospel to the world. They preach about love but describe a god of threats and punishment. These well-mean-

---

65   Luke 5:1-11, Mark 1:16-20 NLT

ing but confused Christians demand that followers join their church, obey their rules, and become like them. They come across to the world as unloving, judgmental, and miserable.

The truth about God's leadership, His law, His Judgment, and His loving character is the answer to our world's problems. In the book of Revelation, Jesus sent three angels with three specific messages right before the end of the world. The messages are hidden in symbols, but when we understand basic principles, the truth is quite easy to see.

The entire book of Revelation has built up to these three messages. To understand them correctly, we must put on the right lenses to get the correct picture of God. If we come to this chapter believing that God is a Dominance leader, that His laws are Imposed laws, and that He is willing to use force to get His way, then the message ignites our fears and pushes us away from Him. It completely destroys our trust in God. But just by looking at the fruits, however, we see that this false view of God comes from evil. If we look at God as a Creator, full of love and freedom, a God who wants intimacy and worship, then we see a completely different message. The three angels become messengers of hope and truth.

Every message from heaven speaks of God's goodness and His love. While these particular messages are unique, they all follow the same theme: God is trustworthy. Moses encouraged us to be still and wait for God's deliverance. Solomon and the temple reminded us to worship. Hosea showed that God will love us forever. Elijah challenged us to get off the fence and choose. Each message was unique and given by different men, but they all echo the call by the sea. We see God's goodness in their stories and words, and we hear Jesus call out, "Follow Me."

The Three Angels' Message is the last message to humanity. It is the final call to follow Him.

The First Angel

The first angel says in a loud voice,
"Fear God and give Him glory
because the hour of His judgment
has come. Worship Him who
made the heavens, the earth, the
seas and the springs of water."[66]

Fear God can mean two things. It can mean *be terrified* or *be amazed*. One version sends us running away from God to hide with Adam and Eve in the bushes. The other calls us to kneel next to Solomon and be still. Only one translation can be correct. Only one draws us closer to God. The very next phrases, *give Him glory* and *worship Him*, speak of wonder and awe. The angel invites us to worship God and see how awesome He truly is.

---

66   Revelation 14:7

Then the angel says this is the hour of His judgment. Who is being judged? Is it us or Him? One belief creates fear as we look at our sinfulness and frantically search for a religious way to escape God's eye. We run and hide behind the cross or try to cover ourselves with Jesus' blood. There are many religious activities designed to protect us from God's punishment. But the problem is not the punishment but the sin.

Sin is separation from God. The last thing we need is a religion that builds barriers between us and God. For all of earth's history, God held out His hand in love. Time is almost up for us to judge God. The third judgment, the one where God accepts our final decision, is about to happen. The door to the ark is about to close. This first message is God's last, desperate attempt to win our hearts.

That is why the message ends by describing God as the Creator. Creation runs on natural laws with natural consequences. He is not a dictator with imposed rules and harsh punishments for those who dare cross Him. God is the Source of Life, and He holds us up with His comforting power. We can trust Him, for He will never control us. His laws are natural and good and support all life. If creation trusts Him, we can too.

The first message is simple. "Look at God and say, 'Wow!' Now is the time to pick a side. Now is the time to choose Him. He is the Creator. His laws show us how reality works. We can trust Him."

The Second Angel

The second angel followed and said,
"Fallen! Fallen is Babylon the Great,
which made all the nations drink the
maddening wine of her adulteries."[67]

The Tower of Babel and Babylon, the city that sprung up in its shadow, represents the opposite ideals of the temple in Jerusalem. It uplifts works over worship. Babylon was a conquering city whose gods demanded sacrifice and perfect obedience. It now symbolizes any religion that resorts to force and violence to make people comply with its version of spirituality. These types of religion are full of confusion and darkness. They pressure people to drink wine that makes them go mad. Wine symbolizes Christ's blood. But this wine is a fraud. It does not bring peace; it brings madness. It is also the wine of adultery. It is a form of religion that turns people away from the true Bridegroom, Jesus. It offers another way to salvation. It promises heaven to those who earn it and become good enough.

The angel warns the world that this system of worship has fallen. The curtain has been ripped apart, and the deception is over. The truth reveals God's character and exposes the lies of false religion. This message is a revelation of truth, not a condemnation of sincere worshippers who have

---

67   Revelation 14:8

been deceived. Good people who have been trying to work their way to heaven or who have been serving God out of fear deserve to know the truth. The great city of false religion is no longer inhabitable. Get out! Come into the light of truth.

Jerusalem is a place of peace where we are loved. We can experience intimacy with God and be completely safe. We can drink the cup of Christ's true blood, which washes away all our fears and selfishness. We can step into a new existence and live in freedom. Everyone is welcome here.

Instead of a harsh judgment, it is a message of hope. The old, dry way of doing religion is over. Everyone who hungers and thirst for righteousness, who longs to be close to Jesus, who wants to live a life of love is invited to step out of the ruins of Babylon and into the vibrant city of God. Babylon, and its false system of worship, has fallen. The sham is over, and the truth is clear.

The first message calls us to look at God's true character and worship. The second message tells us that the lies are over. These two messages bring the truth of God's character to the forefront of humanity. Then everyone chooses.

The Third Angel

The third angel calls out in a loud voice, "If anyone worships the beast and his image and takes his mark on

the forehead or on the hand, he too,
will drink the wine of God's fury,
which has been poured full strength
into the cup of His wrath. He will
be tormented with burning sulfur
in the presence of the holy angels
and of the Lamb. And the smoke
of their torment rises forever and
ever. There is no rest day or night
for those who worship the beast
and his image, or for anyone who
receives the mark of his name."[68]

The last message is a warning. It shows the terrible, natural results of rejecting God. It is not a threat. It is a clear explanation of the consequences to those who cut themselves off from God and invite the demons in.

If we don't understand God's character, then the last message is terrifying. God looks like a furious tyrant who torments people in His presence. But we must remember the truth. God is always good. Look at this message through the sacrificial love of the cross. This message is not a threat; it is a dire warning.

If anyone takes the character of the beast and chooses to live selfishly, then they will drink the wine of God's wrath. The Old Testament tells us

---

68   Based on multiple translations of Revelation 14:9-11

that God's ways are higher than our ways.[69] His emotions run on a different level than ours. Do we think His wrath is like ours? Does God get angry and pitch a holy fit when people are bad, or is there something deeper going on here? We must understand God's wrath.

Paul describes God's wrath in Romans 1 and 2. He writes that "the wrath of God is revealed" against evil men who have rejected every piece of truth sent their way.[70] After they have made their final choice, "God *gave them over* to the sinful desires of their hearts."[71] "God *gave them over* to degrading passions."[72] "God *gave them over* to a depraved mind."[73] God's wrath is giving them over to their sinful hearts and minds. It's letting people go. They reject Him over and over, and finally He stops trying to win them back. He accepts their choice. He is not furious. He is respectful.

The final message says that God's wrath is poured out full strength, and this points to the final letting go. It symbolizes the line in the sand that God will not cross. It means that the rejection of Him is final, and He respects the refusal of His children even though He died for them, even though it breaks His heart.

---

69   Isaiah 55:9

70   Romans 1:18, 2:5

71   Romans 1:24

72   Romans 1:26 NASB

73   Romans 1:28 NIV

Then those who reject God are tormented in the presence of Jesus and the angels. Does this mean that God tortures people as Jesus comes back? Many Christians believe this without seeing the results of the twisted lie. If God is a torturer, then His love crumbles to the dirt and becomes conditional. The teaching that God tortures is from the devil, for it puts the characteristics of evil on God and creates distrust in the hearts of whoever believes that lie.

The torture is a natural result of the rejection. It comes from the choice, not from God. A man who turns out the light causes darkness. He cannot blame the light when he falls into a hole. He chose darkness and its dangers. Every choice has a consequence.

Jesus is coming back. That is a fact. Those who love Him look forward to that wonderful day with joy and hope. But those who don't want anything to do with God and His loving ways will hate being in His presence. Lies hate the truth. Hate cannot stand love. Captivity loathes freedom. When Jesus comes back in His full glory, the truth will shine like never before. No one can pull the wool over their eyes and go back to sleep with the lies. They will see the truths they have rejected. They will feel the love they have spurned, and it will be torture. They have rejected reality, and they loathe the truth.

Jesus will not torture anyone. Those who have chosen to take the character of the beast will writhe in agony because they cannot stand the loving presence of the Lamb.

But the torture begins even before the second coming. Those who choose selfishness immediately step into pain and suffering. We have all experienced this truth. People blame God, when the real culprit is sin. James wrote that when sin is fully grown, it brings death.[74] Sin is the source of pain, suffering, and death. Jesus came to save us from sin, but if we reject Jesus, then sin will destroy us.

Those who make the final decision to follow Jesus will become more and more like Him. Those who choose the beast will become more and more like it. The violence, the greed, the hate, and rage will simmer in the hearts of its followers. Torment does not come from an angry, vengeful God. It comes from a heart of darkness. There is no rest, no peace, no joy for those who choose the beast, who worship a god of force and fear. The third angel's warning is terrifying, but we should fear sin, not God. This message shows us the results of taking the character of the beast—pain, torture, and death. It points us to the only Way out—Jesus.

If anyone worships the beast and values its methods and character traits, then they will become like the beast. They will think and act like the beast. They will completely separate themselves from God's love, and the natural result will be torment. They will hate truth and love so much that being near Jesus will be like torture for them. They will

---

74   James 1:15

have no rest day or night, for there is no cure for selfishness other than God's love.

Message of Hope

After the last message, John writes a quick note of encouragement to those who choose God. "This calls for patient endurance on the part of the saints who obey God's commandments and remain faithful to Jesus."[75]

John doesn't promise an easy way out. He calls believers to be patient and to endure. Then John gives us the key to making it through the last test. "Keep God's commands." This means so much more than following ten rules from Exodus. John heard Jesus break down the commandments to their elemental, eternal truths. John was there when Jesus said, "I give you a new command. Love each other in the same way that I have loved you."[76] John knows that mere rule keeping will not give us the strength to endure. He calls us to commit to a life of love. The greatest commandment tells us to love God and the people in our lives.[77]

Then John calls us to remain faithful to our Savior. Jesus showed the Universe the truth about God. He lived a life of selfless giving, and we remain faithful to Him when we reject any view of God that

---

75   Revelation 14:12

76   Based on multiple translations of John 13:34-35

77   Matthew 22:36-40

contradicts the truth Jesus taught. This is so much more than calling ourselves Christians or going to church. This is about remaining faithful to His character, His commands to love, and His teachings about the Kingdom of Heaven. We cannot follow a god with another character even if it claims the same name as Christ. A good wife knows her partner, and we know Jesus. No one can take His place.

If imposters claim to be Christ, if they perform miracles, if they have supernatural powers, and yet they do not have the character of Jesus, then they are liars. *Antichrist* in Greek means "one who stands in place of."[78] It means adversary, but not a blatant enemy. It is someone who stands in the place of Christ, who pretends to be Christ. The antichrist will not show up as a scary demon. He will be a supernatural being claiming to be Jesus but not having His character of love. True believers will be able to see the difference. Jesus will not persecute those who reject His love. He will not take away their rights to buy and sell. He will not round them up and throw them in jail. He will not kill those who say no to Him. But the Antichrist will. This deceiver will walk and talk like Jesus, but he will resort to force and fear to gain control and power. This is not the spirit of the Lamb. It is the spirit of the beast.

The only way to stand in the end is to patiently endure and wait for God's deliverance. The Lord will

---

78   https://biblehub.com/greek/500.htm

fight for you. You need only to be still.[79] Obey God's commands by loving God first and then loving other people. We must remain faithful to Jesus and His teachings on God's character. The more we focus on Jesus, the more we become like Him. He is our only Safeguard, the Truth, the Life, and the Light at the end of the world.

The Final Truth

Worship the true God. Those who cling to the pagan fables of a controlling god will be miserable. But if we look deeply into the symbols of the temple, the sermons of the prophets, and the stories of Jesus, then we will discover the truth. God is an Influence leader who runs the world through natural law. He wants intimacy with us and gives us the freedom to choose. He created us to worship, and He judged us as worthy. He loves us and has invited us to spend eternity with Him.

The three angels' messages point out the very lies this generation believes about God. These messages speak the truth. They call us into a deeper relationship with God. They warn us that time is almost out. They also call us into action. When we understand how good God is and how it changes everything, we have to share it. How many people are depressed, angry, addicted, greedy, lonely, or hateful. The darkness is so thick, and too many

79   Exodus 14:14

people are running scared because they don't know who God is. They need the light. They need us to share the truth. They need God.

The three angels symbolize God's people on earth during the final days. Their message of hope is the final stanza to the crescendo of God's symphony. The musty religions of rules, works, and force are dead. The three angels warn us of the terrible consequences of choosing the beast over the Lamb. The message calls out the lies and points to the Truth. It holds the keys to unlock the final great deception. It is a roadmap to the end of time. It unveils the true character of God and the terrifying nature of the beast. It shows us the natural results of choosing to accept or reject God's truth. This message must go out. People must decide, because Jesus is coming back soon!

The Groom

This was going to be a great day. Joel had dreamed of this day for years, imagining just how the day would unfold. He would walk up to Hannah's house and find her out back, hanging up clothes to dry in the sun. He would watch her work and marvel at her beauty. Joel couldn't believe that this beautiful woman would soon be his wife. Then he would clear his throat and call her name. Immediately Hannah would turn and run into his arms. He would pick her up, swing her around, and then pull her close.

Joel would gaze into Hannah's deep, brown eyes and whisper the secrets of his heart. She would glow with happiness, and then they would run hand in hand to her father's shop. Soon the wedding celebration would begin.

Joel shook his head and came back from his daydream. He quickened his steps and barely noticed the hot sun on the rocky path. All he saw was blue sky and Hannah's hometown in the valley. It had been twelve long months since he had held her.

Joel remembered back to the first day he'd seen Hannah. He was busy loading the camel for his father when he heard someone scream. He saw a Roman soldier beating an old man. Everyone in the marketplace was too afraid to intervene, so they pretended not to notice.

Suddenly a slender, young woman emerged from the shadows. "Sir! Please stop," she called out. "This man could not see you! Look, he's blind. That's why he ran into you. He meant no harm." She placed a calm hand on the soldier's shoulder.

The Roman's fist froze. He bent down and looked into the old man's face. The soldier huffed and shook his head.

"Well, tell him to be more careful next time," he barked. Then he stood up and stalked out of the marketplace. The girl gently helped the old man stand up, and then the crowd swallowed up the pair. Everyone went back to their business, but not Joel.

He shook his head in amazement at the young woman's bravery and compassion.

His father pointed in her direction and asked, "Who is she?"

Joel smiled. "That's the girl I am going to marry," he said.

Soon the courtship began. After a few awkward conversations, their friendship developed as they slowly shared their hearts and talked of their hopes and dreams. Soon their friendship had blossomed into a deep love. Joel wrote her poems, and Hannah giggled at his bumbling attempts at romance. Joel promised to take care of her as long as he lived. He told Hannah he would go back to his father's town to build their very own house and as soon as it was finished, he would come back for her. Then they would get married and live together forever.

On the last day they were together, Joel promised to return as soon as he could. He gently held Hannah's hands and asked her if she would wait for him.

"How long will you be gone?" Hannah asked.

"I don't know, Beloved," Joel answered. "Maybe months. Maybe a year. It depends on a lot of things."

"Will you visit me?" she asked.

"No, but not because I don't want to. I just have to spend every free moment I can working on our new home so we can begin our new life together as soon as possible." Joel's eyes sparkled with excitement. "Will you wait for me?"

Hannah looked up at him, and his heart melted. Joel would do anything for this woman. Hannah smiled, "Of course, I will."

Joel cupped her face in his hands and whispered, "I will love you forever."

The Return

That was twelve months ago, and finally Joel entered the gates of her small town. He passed the synagogue and took the shortcut behind some cattle stalls. He walked through the square where he had first seen Hannah and down the street that led to her house. Joel knocked on the front door, but no one answered.

He smiled and thought, *I bet she's in the back, hanging laundry.* Joel briskly walked around the house grinning from ear to ear, but an unexpected sound stopped him cold.

He heard laughter, but it wasn't the giggle of girls doing their chores. Joel heard a man and woman talking, teasing, giggling. He recognized Hannah's voice, but not the man's. That voice sounded young, confident, and strong.

Joel spun around the corner and stopped dead still. Hannah stood next to a handsome young man. He was holding a basket of wet clothes, and she playfully smacked him with a wet tunic and pinned it to the line. The man leaned toward Hannah and murmured something, then she burst out loud laughing. Hannah was so happy, but she was with another man.

She didn't wait for me, Joel thought. His shoulders slumped, and his heart broke. This was nothing like his dreams. Joel stood frozen, unable to tear his eyes away from Hannah. Smiling, she put her hand on the man's strong shoulder. Joel shook his head as his mind raced. *She promised to wait*! he thought in a panic.

Hannah reached down for another wet cloak and suddenly saw Joel. She cried out in joy and started to run to him, but then she stopped. Hannah saw Joel's look of betrayal. She frowned, because at first she didn't understand his confusion. Then in a flash of realization, Hannah looked back at the handsome man standing next to the laundry.

"Cousin," she called out. "Come meet Joel, my future husband."

Then Hannah ran and leaped into Joel's arms. It took him a few moments to realize what she meant.

"He's your cousin?" Joel stammered.

Hannah kissed his cheek, "Yes, my love." Then she held his face in her hands and looked deeply into Joel's eyes. "I waited for you, because I love you."

Joel touched Hannah's forehead with his. "Thank you," he whispered. "I'm so glad you waited!" Then Joel smiled and promised, "I will love you forever."

The Second Coming

Not all bridegrooms returned to find their lovers faithful, waiting patiently for their return. Some devastated young men found their fiances with another man. Their impatient brides had not waited but had chosen someone else.

Our Bridegroom is coming back. He has almost finished our new home and will return very soon. What will Jesus find when He returns for His beloved? Will He find us faithfully waiting or in the arms of another god, distracted, and surprised? He already made His choice. Now it is up to us.

The time to decide is now, yet many have not made their final decision. They are hesitating. They hold back because they are afraid. The Three Angels' Message takes away the fear. It shows God as the Creator. It describes His laws as natural laws. It shows the results of rejection and gives humanity the freedom to decide. The entire Bible points to the truth: God is good. He is trustworthy. He loves us.

Before we can share this good news, we must first encounter Jesus. The good news is that He is already waiting for us.

Your Turn

You are standing at the edge of the water. You can feel the coarse sand in between your toes and hear the birds call out in the crisp morning air. The sun peeks over the distant hills, and the calm water sparkles. The beach is deserted, and you take a deep breath and close your eyes.

Then you hear footsteps. Someone is walking down the beach. You turn and squint into the morning sunlight. The Man senses you and stops. He turns and looks into your eyes.

Your heart leaps into your throat. It's Jesus! Somehow you just know it. He nods and smiles, but He holds your gaze. For a brief moment, everything freezes. The water, the breeze, and the birds fade away as all you see is Him. His eyes dance, and the corners of His mouth hide a smile. You can feel Jesus reading your soul. He sees your sins. He feels your pain. He knows your heart's desire. You are completely exposed and vulnerable, but somehow you still feel safe. Then Jesus can't hold it in any longer, and a warm smile bursts upon His face.

"Follow Me," Jesus says. Then He turns and walks into the sunlight. You hesitate. You think. You doubt. But you can't take your eyes off of Him. Jesus looks over His shoulder and waves for you to catch up. Every fiber of your soul longs to run after Him, but something holds you back. It's fear.

If you follow Him, you'll have to trust Him. You'll have to believe that He is good, that He can take care of you, that He will save you. You will have to let go of so many things.

Jesus stops and turns around again. The look in His face says that He understands your fear, but at the same time you can feel His love. It's warm and fresh and free. Suddenly, you realize that all your life you have been searching for that love, and now here He is.

Jesus holds out a hand and motions for you to come. "Come to Me," He says kindly. "Let Me heal you. Let Me give you peace. Let Me make you fearless."

You smile and take the first step.

The Beginning

Main Points: I am fearless because ...
God is good.
God gives me the freedom to follow Him or walk away.
God is calling me to share the truth about Him.
God is with me.

ACKNOWLEDGMENTS

"All of us have special someones
who have loved us into being."
— Fred Rogers

Riley, you are my dream come true, my best friend, and the best wife in the world. Thank you for believing in me, supporting my dreams, and never giving up on me. You are special to me, and I love you just the way you are.

Libby, you are brave and strong. You are beautiful and good. Your mommy and daddy and Jesus love you very much. Thank you for teaching me so much about God's love as you giggle and tickle your way through my life.

Mom and Dad, you see something in me that no one else sees. Thank you for listening to me, encouraging me, and loving me when it was hard. You are truly great gifts from God.

Aunt Nancy, thank you for investing hours and hours in helping me edit this book. Your suggestions have truly sparked life into the stories, and your comments have pushed me to write on a deeper level than I ever could have by myself. Thank you.

Sean Maycock, you are a true friend. Some of the best memories of my life happened with you on Saipan. Thank you for mentoring me as a young teacher and showing me how to be a good man. Your insights and different perspectives have given me the gift of seeing the world through your eyes. Strength and Honor, my friend.

Mr. Roberts, the very first book I ever wrote was in your classroom. You will never know how much you have impacted my life. I can still hear you say, "Find a way to get it done," and "If you don't have time to do it right the first time, when will you find time to do it right again?" Both mantras have helped me during this project. Thank you.

Dr. Byrd, I greatly respect your wisdom, knowledge, and character. Your influence helped shape me into the man I am today. Thank you for your help on this book.

Gary, you have been a great writing coach. Your guidance helped me burst through the obstacles and come to the finish line. Thank you.

Sky, you have been a terrific editor. Thank you for your attention to detail and encouraging words.

ABOUT THE AUTHOR

Grant Graves is an international speaker and author. He is a master storyteller who believes that Jesus is coming back soon.

Too many people are afraid of that wonderful day, and Grant's passion is to share the truth about God's good character so people can enjoy a fearless life.

Grant loves travel, exercise, great books, his wonderful family.

WHAT'S NEXT?

If you would like to join the Fearless tribe, look Grant Graves up on Facebook or Youtube. Check out his free content and sign up for the free companion journal to *Fearless*, by going to grantngraves.com

Grant Graves speaks at churches, schools, and other religious gatherings. To book a keynote or seminar email grant@grantngraves.com

YOU ARE AWESOME!

Thank you for reading my book!

I really appreciate your feedback,
and I love hearing what you have to say.

I need your input to make the next version
of this book and my future books even better.
Please leave a helpful review on Amazon
letting me know what you thought of the book.

Thank you so much!
— Grant Graves

Made in the USA
Coppell, TX
17 January 2021

47313717R00152